COLLECTING
THINGS

OTHER BOOKS BY PAUL VILLIARD

Insects as Pets
Reptiles as Pets
Exotic Fish as Pets
Wild Mammals as Pets
Through the Seasons with a Camera
Jewelry Making
Collecting Stamps
Birds as Pets

Paul Villiard

★★★★★★★★★★★★★

COLLECTING THINGS

with photographs by the author

Doubleday & Company, Inc.
GARDEN CITY, NEW YORK

For Paul and William

Library of Congress Cataloging in Publication Data
Villiard, Paul.
    Collecting things.

    SUMMARY: Describes the many unusual things that people collect and gives, wherever possible, the history of each particular collection.
    1. Collectors and collecting—Juvenile literature.
[1. Collectors and collecting] I. Title.
AM231.V54   790.13
ISBN 0-385-07054-3 Trade
    0-385-08018-2 Prebound
Library of Congress Catalog Card Number 74-34181

Copyright © 1975 by Gertrude Villiard as Exectrix of the
    Estate of Paul Villiard
All Rights Reserved
Printed in the United States of America
FIRST EDITION

CONTENTS

Chapter one		Paper Americana	*1*
Section	*1*	Bookplates	*3*
Section	*2*	Theater Programs	*5*
Section	*3*	Company Receipts	*9*
Section	*4*	Trade Cards	*10*
Section	*5*	Postal Cards	*13*
Section	*6*	Advertising Leaflets	*16*
Section	*7*	Railroad Material	*18*

Section 8	Pre-adhesive Postage	20
Section 9	Transportation Leaflets	23
Section 10	Newspapers	25
Section 11	Communication Items	27
Chapter two	Bag Labels	30
Chapter three	Cigar Bands	34
Chapter four	Soap Wrappers	37
Chapter five	Automobile Plates	39
Chapter six	Bottles	43
Chapter seven	Insulators	48
Chapter eight	Keys	52
Chapter nine	Match Book Covers	56
Chapter ten	Sugar Wrappers	61
Chapter eleven	Buttons	65
Chapter twelve	Posters	69
Chapter thirteen	Picture Post Cards	71
Chapter fourteen	Campaign Buttons	75
Chapter fifteen	Barbed Wire	78
Chapter sixteen	Stamps	82
Chapter seventeen	Coins	85
Chapter eighteen	Travel Decals	90
Chapter nineteen	Buttonhooks	93
Chapter twenty	Shoulder Patches	96
Chapter twenty-one	Bookmarks	99
Chapter twenty-two	Spoons	102
Chapter twenty-three	Bubble Gum Items	105
Chapter twenty-four	Toy Soldiers	107
Chapter twenty-five	Autographs	110
Chapter twenty-six	Thimbles	112
Chapter twenty-seven	A List of Things People Collect	115

PREFACE

The study of animal behavior is a fascinating occupation, and the deeper one gets into it, the more a person wants to learn. Some of the things animals do are really astonishing. When we think of animal behavior, we usually think of the ways of all animals other than ourselves. But certainly people are as much animals as are cats, dogs, elephants, or wombats. The only trouble is, that most people think of themselves as the *noblest* animal that ever trod the earth.

Well, we won't get into a discussion of this assumed nobility, but, rather, we'll take a look at some of the things human beings do that are very similar to some of the things other animals do.

In the vastness of Asia, small animals called gerbils are great hoarders. In the western part of our own country are a species of rat which does much the same thing—hoards away collections of things, most of which are of no earthly use to the animal. They are variously called pack rats, trader rats, or hoarding rats. The story goes that the rat steals some object from a camper, to cart off to its burrow, but when it does so, it always leaves something in exchange—a pebble, or bit of twig, or some other equally useless object.

Actually, the probable explanation of all this is that the rat has something in its mouth, found during its foraging for food, and in the act of returning to its burrow stumbles across a campsite. Seeing a bright object, the rat seizes the eye-catching item, dropping whatever it was carrying in the process. Many many animals are attracted to bright objects. Fish will investigate every time when a flashing metal "spoon" is trawled through the water, finally grabbing it in their mouth, to their instant distress, because, hidden by the attractive flash of metal, is a dull-colored hook which, yanked through the poor creature's lower lip, soon lands it into the proverbial frying pan.

Preface

Preface

Birds are especially fond of pecking at shiny things, and cage birds in particular will spend hours on end batting at a tiny bell hung from the bars, as much to see the flash as to hear the tinkle. A mirror will hold a little budgie enthralled, to the point of hypnotism, it would seem.

But by far, the most popular occupation of animals is the hoarding of objects, whether they be bits of food, which has some sense to it after all, to twigs, pebbles, and bits of human refuse, which makes no sense at all. They collect these things because, evidently, the amassing of a hoard gives them a feeling of security. Linus and his blanket.

And people are no exception. As a matter of fact, people are the champion hoarders of all time. Never has there been such a race of pack rats as the human race, and never has there been so great a variety of useless things collected with ambition and tenacity. Once the collecting bug hits a person he is sunk. From then on, his only thought is to acquire as much or as many of that particular item as it is humanly possible to do.

The value of the things collected seems to have little to do with the matter. True, many subjects are valuable, or, rather, other people, similarly bitten by the collecting bug, are more than willing to pay out large sums of money for each individual specimen of whatever is being collected by another. This places the value on an article, otherwise useless. Take railroad timetables, as an example. Now I ask you, what earthly use has an old railroad timetable to anybody? Especially since the railroad

Preface

which issued the timetable probably went out of business anywhere from twenty-five to seventy-five years ago. The tracks are long torn up, and the right-of-way is now under some gigantic swimming pool belonging to a chain motel or maybe forming the base for a shopping mall. No one living even remembers that a railroad used to smoke up the landscape, huffing and puffing its lonely way along the course. Yet I have seen an old railroad timetable which the owner refused to sell for over one hundred dollars. Wow!

I must confess that I am no exception to this strange animal behavior. From childhood I have been a collector. First, I collected cigar bands. I still have a part of my very extensive collection of these colorful and useless bits of paper that are wrapped around a cigar as a way of advertising the product. They were to be had for the picking up. Cigar smokers usually purchased the cigar, slid the band off, dropping it to the street, and went their way puffing contentedly on the noxious smoke, not realizing, and probably not caring about what they were doing to their lungs and general health. (It's only recently that my friend, the Surgeon General of the United States, has been trying to warn them.) Also, not caring about the litter they were contributing to in the discarding of the band.

I cared even less, I'm afraid, haunting cigar store doorways after school waiting for the emerging customer to add to my ever-growing hoard of "valuable" cigar bands. Friends of my father brought them to me from Europe.

Other friends whose fathers worked in cigar factories, smuggled out uncut bands in sheets as they came from the printer—these being comparable to imperforate errors in postage stamp collecting. I was the cigar band king of my neighborhood, and, I was certain, of the entire section of the country.

All of which just goes to show that anything, anything at all, is worth something to someone, no matter how useless you or I may think it is. On the other hand, some things people collect are very valuable to everybody—not just to the person collecting them. And these things take time, consideration, and money to achieve a good collection.

This book is designed to tell you about some of the things people collect. Many of these collections are very worthwhile. Many of them are not. The value of some of the things is just what the person owning them puts on it. The value of others is very real, and the articles are worth the same to everybody—not just to the collector.

At any rate, you should find the list interesting, since it presents a cross section of human nature as well as hints on what to collect.

Enjoy.

Preface

Paul Villiard
Saugerties, New York

COLLECTING THINGS

Chapter one

Paper Americana

★★★★★★★★★★★★★★★★★★★★★★

Paper Americana

In the art of collecting things, some items have an interesting historical background as well as an intrinsic value. Perhaps the history is national. Perhaps local. Naturally, local history appeals only to those persons living in that area, rather than to the general public.

I am indebted to Mr. Robert Harris of Wynantskill, New York, for the material on Paper Americana included in this book. Mr. Harris is by way of being an authority on local historical items, and deals in them as well.

One place to collect these things is an old garret or cellar where you can pore through the bundles of papers usually stored there. Old empty houses are wonderful places to explore in the search for papers, but be sure you have permission to go into such places. Also, be careful of rotting floor beams, which, if stepped upon accidentally, might just send you into the cellar before you have completed your search in the attic.

Another good place to look for paper items is in secondhand bookstores. Many a choice paper has been placed between the pages of an old book and long forgotten. While searching through the old books, you may also come upon one with a bookplate in it.

Paper Americana

Section 1

BOOKPLATES

The collecting of bookplates is a bonafide hobby, but one which used to carry a certain stigma attached to it. This stigma was connected with the removal of a bookplate from a book. The bookplate, on being fastened inside the flyleaf of a book, became part of that book, and the removal of the plate constituted deformation of the volume.

Bookplate collecting carries with it a study of people. Usually the designs on bookplates—some of them are very ornate and perfectly beautiful examples of the engraver's art—were the arms and heraldry of the person owning the book. If the family had not traced its own lineage, then bookplates were available bearing a conventional type of coat-of-arms with no family attachments. Under the design is usually a block inside which the owner inscribed his or her name. More affluent persons had their names engraved or printed in this space. Others merely wrote them in.

Paper Americana

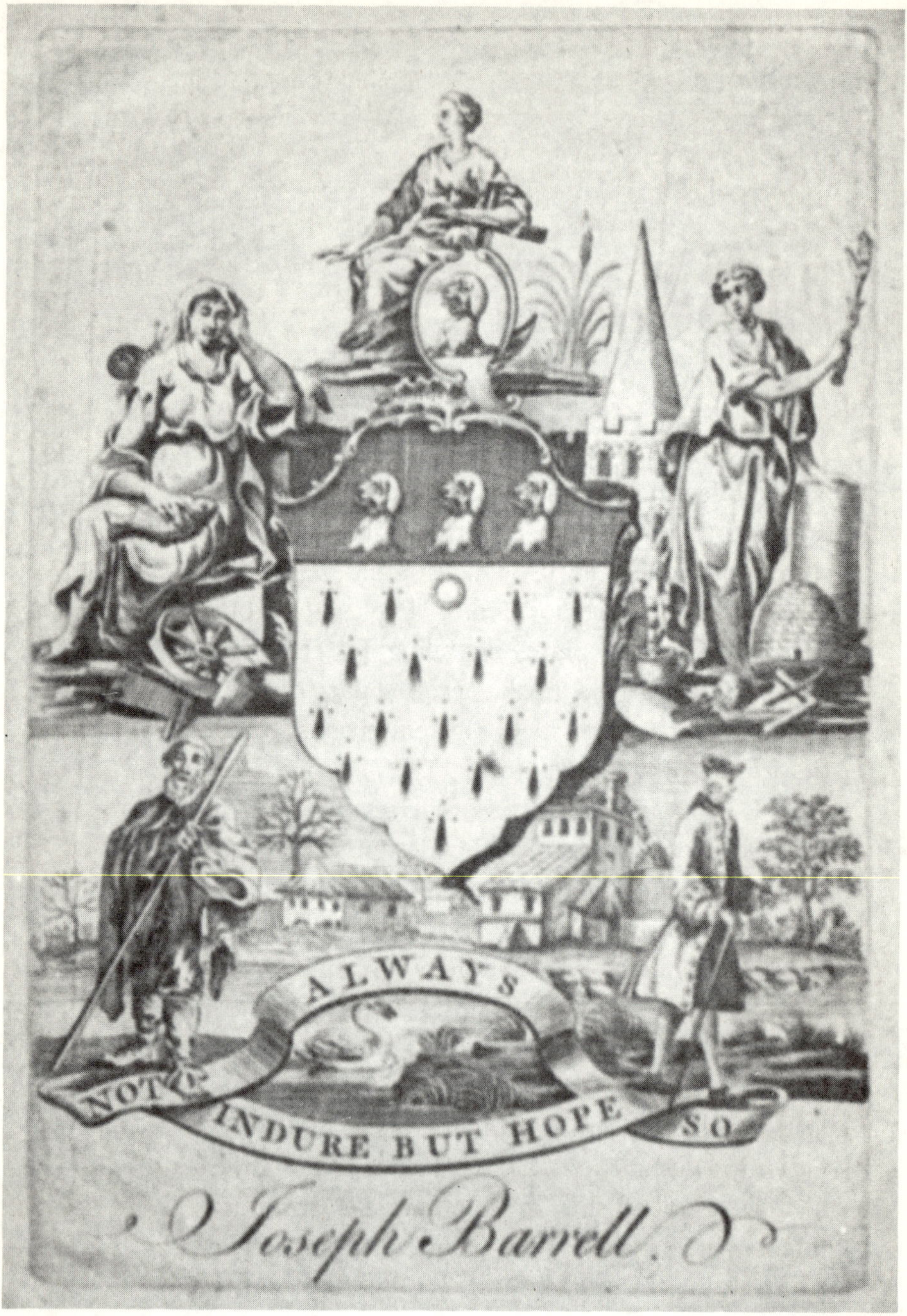
ALWAYS
NOT INDURE BUT HOPE SO
Joseph Barrell

To start a collection of bookplates, one can purchase them from dealers in paper items for a very small amount. Then, after you have the nucleus of a collection, you may hunt them out for yourself. You may have friends who use bookplates themselves, and could give you one, preferably used, since that makes the item more authentic.

Section 2
THEATER PROGRAMS

These are collected by a great number of people, for a great number of reasons. First, if you go to the theater often, you might like to make a collection of the programs of all the plays you went to see. If you seldom go, the collecting of the programs has an even greater significance for you, since they indicate landmarks in your leisure time that are pleasant to recall when rereading the programs. Performers also collect programs because programs deal with their particular interests.

Most theater programs carry advertising of one kind or another, and some people like to collect programs for the ads. There is often an index of local establishments and the wares

Paper Americana

PROGRAM

Kennedy
Sporting and Mufti Tailor
292 FIFTH AVENUE

GOLD MEDAL, PARIS 1900

The conventional Dress suit for the opera season, in a new weave and shade of "indigo blue," one of London's latest (though the standard black will always be good form), will be more artistic than ever before, with a single breasted waistcoat, "V" shaped opening, made of embroidered material in various tints.

The Tuxedo or Dinner jacket is made of an indistinct striped gray and black undressed worsted.

As an adjunct to the evening dress, we mention the Opera coat, our own creation, of lamb's wool in black and seal brown.

PATTERNS OF SELF MEASUREMENT MAILED ON REQUEST

Note.—Gentlemen will kindly refr... that it seriously interferes with the sing...

JOSEPH WEBER p...
Weber's T...
in DREA...

A Dramatic "Pip...
Dialogue and Lyrics by Edgar S...
PRODUCED UNDER THE STAGE
MUSIC UNDER DIRECTION O...

CHARA...

WILHELM DINGLEBENDER ...
J. BILKINGTON HOLMES ...
HENRI D'ABSINTHE ...
SETH HUBBS ...
HENRY PECK ...
WILLIE PECK ..... His restles...
OLD MAN PLATT ...
JOE SNEDIKER
HANK SCUDDER } ... Villag...
HEN CONKLIN
BIG BILL HANKINS ...
NANCY ...

Continued on...

WILSON That's All

" • THE • PLAY

...from smoking, as it has been found
...ng of the Company.

...fers at this Performance

...heatre Co.

...M CITY

...e" in Two Puffs

...nith. Music by Victor Herbert

...DIRECTION OF AL. HOLBROOK

...OF LOUIS F. GOTTSCHALK

...CTERS

..., Long Island truck farmer, with a
...eamy disposition and a chronic
...stanse for labor ...... JOE WEBER
..., Real Estate boomer, with the
...ams of an ideal city
OTIS HARLAN
... artist seeking rural atmosphere
MAURICE FARKOA
...illage hackman and the oracle of
...Malaria Center . . WILL T. HODGE
..., city flat-dweller, spending the
...eek-end with his family in the
...untry .... W. L. ROMAINE
...ffspring, LILLIAN FITZGERALD
... relic .... MAJOR JOHNSON
...Romeos { W. D. STEVENSON / ERNEST WOOD / JAMES McCORMACK
..., farm hand .... WILL LODELLA
...Ringlebender's daughter and the
...lle of Malaria Center
CECILIA LOFTUS

...llowing page

"When you do drink, drink Trimble"

To Our Guests!

"You are very welcome to our house:
It must appear in other ways than words."
—*Shakespeare.*

Trimble
Whiskey
Green Label

At all First-Class Dealers

WHITE, HENTZ & Co., Phil. & N. Y.
Sole Proprietors. Established 1793.

Ned Wayburn's TRAINING SCHOOL FOR THE STAGE

PRACTICAL INSTRUCTIONS BY THE MOST SUCCESSFUL STAGE DIRECTOR IN THE WORLD

STAGE-DANCING, ACTING, "MAKE-UP," COSTUMING, Etc.

Classes for adults and children; over 3000 pupils in public now. Special course for vaudeville. Young men taught stage management. Engagement contracts given all graduates at from $25.00 to $50.00 per week. References any reputable theatrical manager, critic, actor, actress or chorus girl. Address:

NED WAYBURN, 115 WEST 42nd STREET, NEW YORK

they advertise. It is very nostalgic to go through a collection of old theater programs and read the advertising in them, comparing the things sold then with those sold in the present. Comparing, also, the prices, some of which will seem ridiculous by their small amounts. Truly, theater programs almost more than any other kind of souvenir, carry perfect examples of the phrase, "Them days is gone forever!"

In collecting theater programs, there is a distinction between the various kinds. Programs issued for orchestral concerts or musical recitals fall into one category. Those dealing with stage plays, another. Even some of the larger movie houses used to issue programs. Besides the program material, the early periods of technological development within the theater, stage, or movies are of special interest to some people, and the old programs do bring these developments to the attention of their collector.

Look for them in attics, cellars, boxes of old papers, empty houses, and similar locations.

Paper Americana

Section 3

COMPANY RECEIPTS

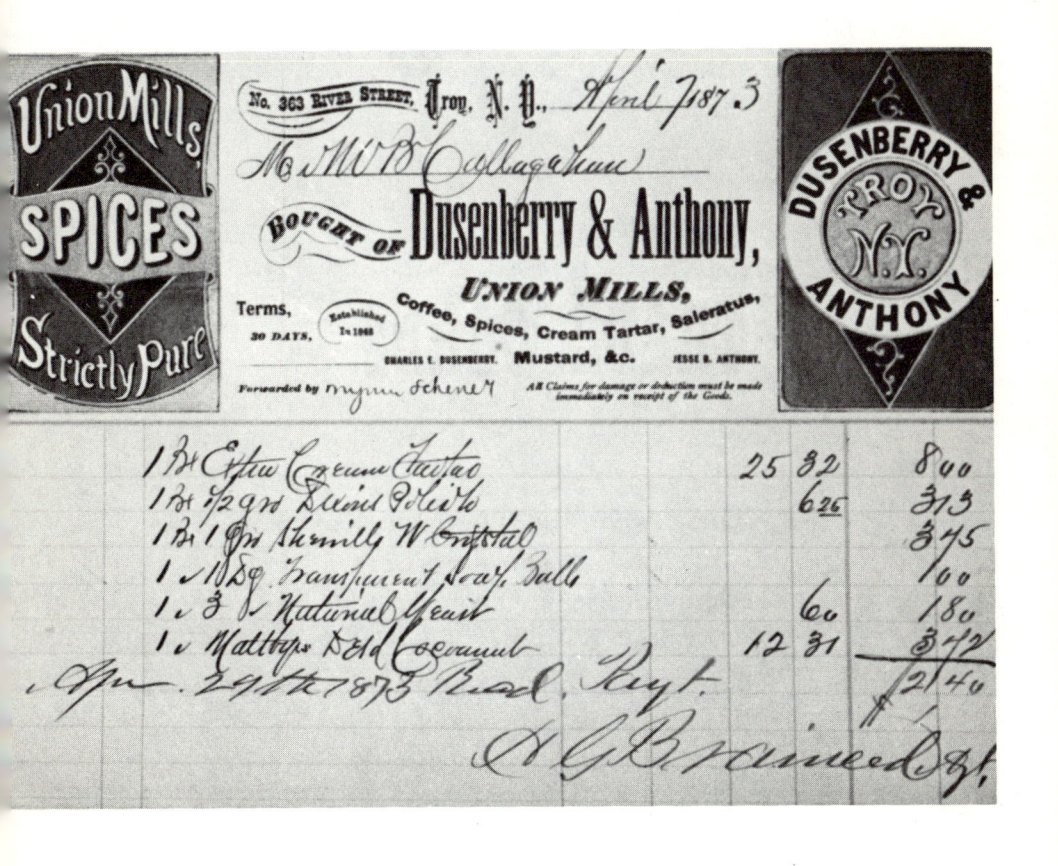

At first thought, company receipts seem to be an item lacking in interest to anyone. But this is not the case if you have a love of fine engraving and art work. Some of the old receipts used by store proprietors in the early days were magnificent works, resplendent with color and intricate engraving. Some of them had worked the coat-of-arms of the storekeeper into the heading design. Others illustrated one or more of the items he sold or manufactured. Mainly of local interest, a collection of company receipts can cover the history of your home town from the very beginning.

The larger the company, usually the better their receipts and letterheads. I have seen these items bearing beautiful works of lithography, which, today, are unheard of because of the enormous cost of reproduction.

Section 4

TRADE CARDS

Paper Americana

These were the forerunners of picture post cards, and at one time were in great vogue. Almost every merchant had trade cards printed which carried scenes depicting and identifying a particular brand of merchandise for which the merchant was known. These trade cards were produced nationally by larger manu-

PEOPLES LINE STEAMERS

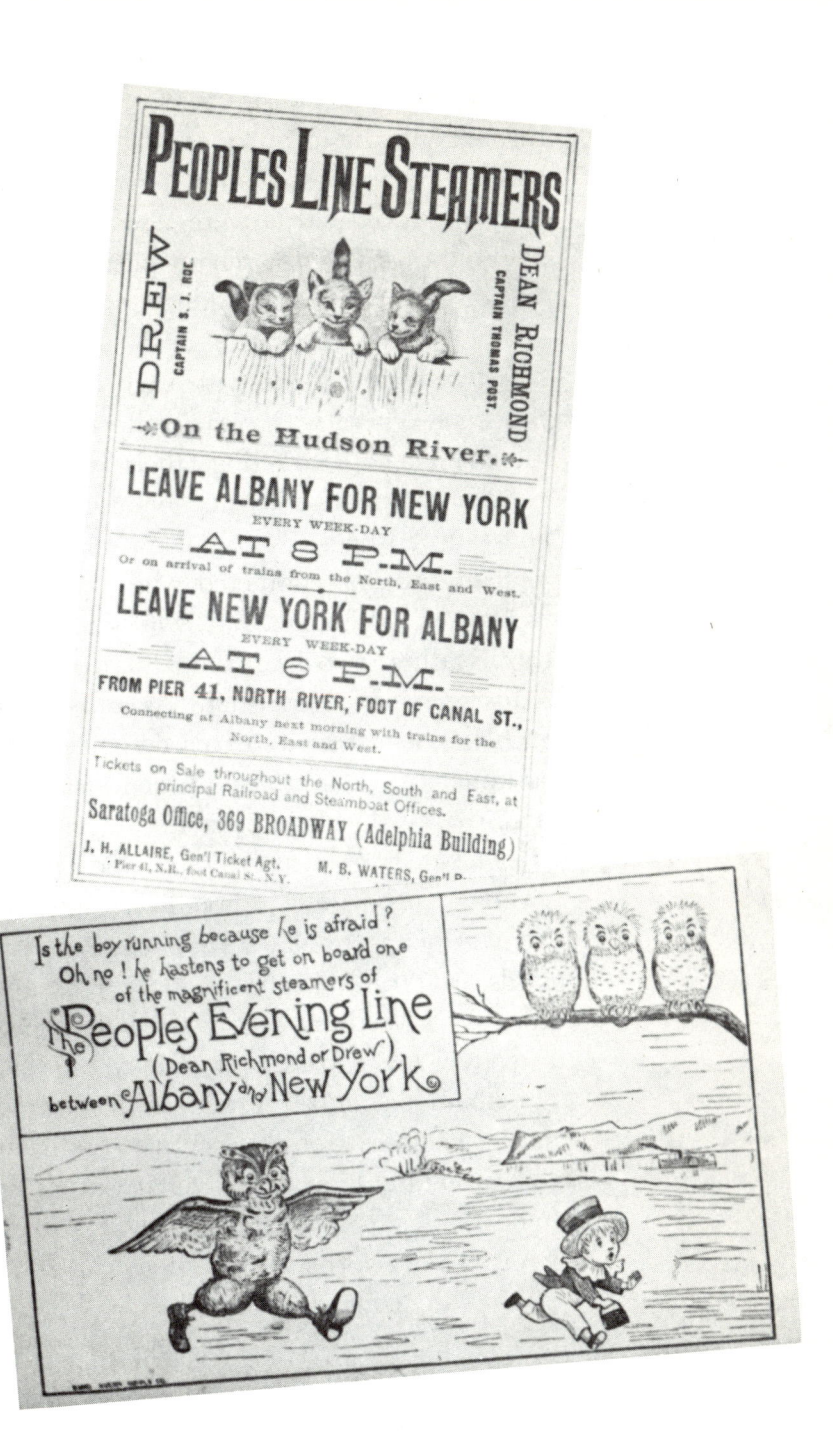

DREW — CAPTAIN S. J. ROE.

DEAN RICHMOND — CAPTAIN THOMAS POST.

On the Hudson River.

LEAVE ALBANY FOR NEW YORK
EVERY WEEK-DAY
AT 8 P.M.
Or on arrival of trains from the North, East and West.

LEAVE NEW YORK FOR ALBANY
EVERY WEEK-DAY
AT 6 P.M.
FROM PIER 41, NORTH RIVER, FOOT OF CANAL ST.,
Connecting at Albany next morning with trains for the North, East and West.

Tickets on Sale throughout the North, South and East, at principal Railroad and Steamboat Offices.

Saratoga Office, 369 BROADWAY (Adelphia Building)

J. H. ALLAIRE, Gen'l Ticket Agt.
Pier 41, N.R., foot Canal St., N.Y.
M. B. WATERS, Gen'l D.

Is the boy running because he is afraid? Oh no! he hastens to get on board one of the magnificent steamers of the **Peoples Evening Line** (Dean Richmond or Drew) between Albany and New York

facturers, and distributed to merchants throughout the country, with the individual names and addresses added to the cards. Locally produced cards were also issued, associated only with the merchant putting them out, and depicting only his products.

Usually the trade cards were included by way of advertising with each order leaving the store. There was great competition among merchants in marketing their wares. Even greater competition existed between steamship and railroad lines. By this, I do not mean that a steamship line competed with a railroad for passengers, although that was sometimes the case. Rather, two steamship lines or two railroads were in competition. As a consequence, each line issued trade cards designed to entice customers to their transportation system rather than that of their competitor.

Nowhere was this competition more severe than on the Hudson River lines, plying from Albany to New York City, and trade cards, full of advertising gimmicks, are obtainable advertising rate wars and other ways to convince the passenger that this is the line he should patronize. Trade cards petered out at the beginning of this century, and now are to be found only in musty cellars, attics, in the hands of collectors, and in dealers of paper items. They are the subject of special collectors all over the country.

Paper Americana

Section 5

POSTAL CARDS

These cards differ from post cards in that the latter are printed by anyone who wishes to make them, while postal cards are the official card issued by the government for purposes of sending short messages through the mail at a rate reduced from letter rates.

Postal card collecting is usually practiced by philatelists—stamp collectors—but there are thousands of persons collecting government postal cards who have no interest in stamps, nor any real knowledge of stamp collecting.

The first postal cards were issued in Austria in 1869. Prior to this time the only way of communication was by letter. Letter communication was very formalized, and the postal rate was very high. Emanuel Herman, an economics professor in Vienna, proposed a card upon which a short note could be written and which would be carried at a reduced rate. It met with great response, and several other countries soon followed suit and issued postal cards of their own. Soon the formula card was

Paper Americana

issued. This one had the stamp printed right on the card, and was sold by the post offices as an item—the card, and the stamp.

The early postal cards were inscribed, WRITE THE ADDRESS ON THIS SIDE—THE MESSAGE ON THE OTHER. This inscription was printed on the face of the card. Later, in view of the fact that people often wrote more than the card could conveniently hold, and so turned the card over and continued their message on the address side, making it difficult to pick the name and address of the recipient out of the maze of writing, the inscriptions were changed to read, NOTHING BUT THE ADDRESS CAN BE PLACED ON THIS SIDE. Finally, in 1892, a kind of double card was issued. This consisted of two postal cards, attached along one edge by a rouletted line to make it easy to separate the two. Both cards had a stamp on them, and one was inscribed MESSAGE CARD the other, REPLY CARD. Both carried the additional inscription THIS SIDE OF CARD IS FOR ADDRESS ONLY.

Postal card collections are made either for the card itself, usually by a stamp collector, or for the person to whom the card was sent—if it were a famous person—or for the person who sent the card, if he were famous. The cards are also collected for the messages they contain, if of historical or personal interest. Often companies will purchase postal cards in large uncut sheets of forty, having the sheets printed with their private advertising for mailing lists.

Paper Americana

The availability of postal cards in full uncut sheets soon led to the unethical and dishonest practice of cutting the cards in such a manner that the stamp was located in a different position than normal. These were sold by unscrupulous persons for enormous prices as "cutting errors" and the swindle is still going on for the unwary. I should advise any collector of postal cards to beware of any he may come across with the stamp misplaced.

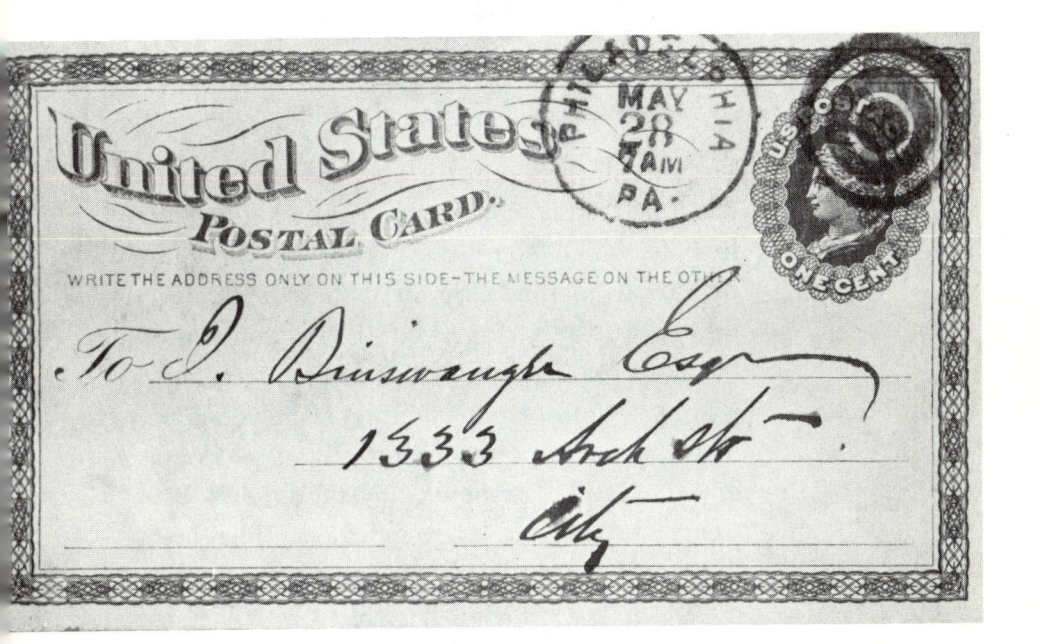

Section 6

ADVERTISING LEAFLETS

During the last century and the early part of this one, many companies printed advertising leaflets which were distributed to the public by various methods. Some of these leaflets were very beautifully engraved. They constitute a branch of collecting that is most interesting as a cross section of our commercial development. These items are often found among old papers in attics and basements, in secondhand bookstores, and at old paper dealers. The leaflet illustrated is for the advertising of bicycles.

Paper Americana

Bicycles used to be called hobby horses, and the early ones were a real hazard to ride. They had enormous front wheels, and tiny rear wheels, and the pedals were directly connected to the front hub. These kinds were in vogue during the 1880s and the 1890s, after which the hobby horse began a series of mechanical innovations, finally resulting in having the wheels the same size, and having the power

RAMBLER NUMBER FOURTEEN.

Weight, 22 pounds.   For lady, 20 pounds.

$100

Edward Clarence Clark agt
Esperance N.Y.

delivered to the vehicle through a pair of sprockets and a chain, with the rear wheel receiving the power instead of the front. Finally the bicycle has been developed into the ten-speed gear-shifting machine as we now know it.

This particular advertising cover is most interesting, since it announces the bicycle at a price of $100.00. The leaflet was published in 1890. This price is phenomenal, since, when the Ford Motor Car Company began selling their gasoline-powered automobiles, the price of one was only about $200.00.

The cover of the catalogue of which this leaflet is but one page had a marvelous engraving depicting an Indian throwing his leg over a bicycle, ready to ride off, while to one side lay his horse, an arrow through its heart, with the bow and quiver lying alongside the unfortunate creature!

Paper Americana

Section 7

RAILROAD MATERIAL

This is a very popular category of paper collecting, and, together with other transportation items, one that gives an excellent picture of the development of our country. Old timetables, tickets, passes, and advertising literature from the many railroad companies are always in demand. Streetcar transfers are very popular items, too. Most streetcar companies issued transfers on payment of the fare. These passes permitted the passenger to change from the car he mounted to another car going to another destination within the city. In this way the passenger was able to journey to his home without paying separate fares on the two different car lines. Of course, both lines were a part of the same transportation company. In some cities, however, transfers were issued from one line to another, the two companies having a reciprocal system permitting the passenger to make trips otherwise impossible on the surface transit lines.

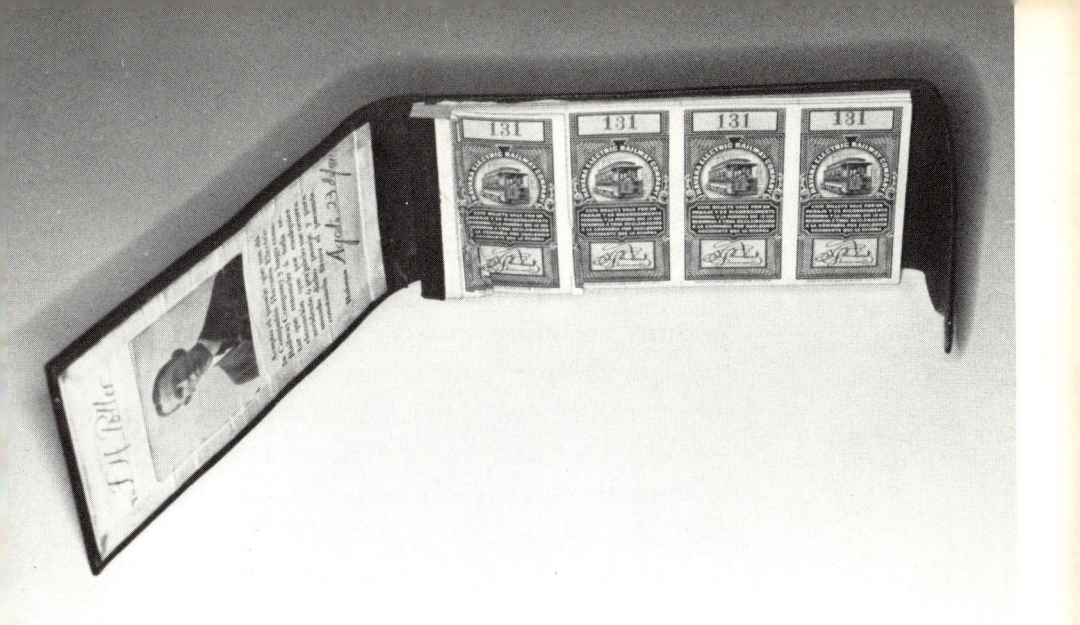

The book of passes shown here was issued in Cuba by the Cuban-Havana Rail System. It serves as an item collectible in two

Paper Americana

19

separate categories—that of railway and surface transportation items, of course, and in the category of American Banknote Company material. The American Banknote Company is a security printing company, printing tickets, stamps, and paper money, as well as stocks and bond certificates, for countries all over the world. A great many people collect material printed by this firm as a special kind of item, and the passes shown are an example, although not one of the best from the point of view of beauty. They were probably passes issued to an employee or official of the company. The photograph being a form of identification for the owner, authenticating the passes when offered for transportation.

Paper Americana

Section 8
PRE-ADHESIVE POSTAGE

The first adhesive postage stamps were issued in 1840 by Great Britain. The first in the United States were issued in 1847. Prior to that time letters were sent without stamps, but with the cost of transportation written on the envelope or folded page. Unlike our present system of charging postage by the weight of the article, postage was charged by the number of pages sent, and by this illogical system of rating, the envelope counted as a page, too. For this reason many letters were merely folded sheets of paper on the inside of which the letter was written.

Besides the number of pages, the distance the letter had to travel was a postal rate consideration, and anything enclosed within the letter was also counted as a page by the postal clerk. Since the postmaster was paid according to the amount of postage he collected, he resorted to all sorts of dodges to try to collect the maximum amount of postage from the customer.

Conversely, the customers resorted to all kinds of dodges to circumvent the high postal rates. A letter, for example, would be written to two different people, with instructions for the first recipient to cut the sheet in two and deliver the other half to the friend. In this way, two letters were sent as one.

Also, during that time—the early 1800s—currency, especially specie, or metal coinage, was of many different kinds. According to the treasurer's report of 1830, of the $24,000,000 in specie in circulation in the United States, $14,000,000 were in United States coinage; $5,000,000 in Spanish coinage; $3,000,000 in the coins of Great Britain, and the rest in the coinage of several different countries. In some areas, foreign coinage was all that was in circulation—mostly of British

Paper Americana

or Spanish money, and the value of these foreign coins were such that the national equivalent was 6¼ cents, or 12½ cents. As a consequence letter rates were supposed to be paid in foreign coinage.

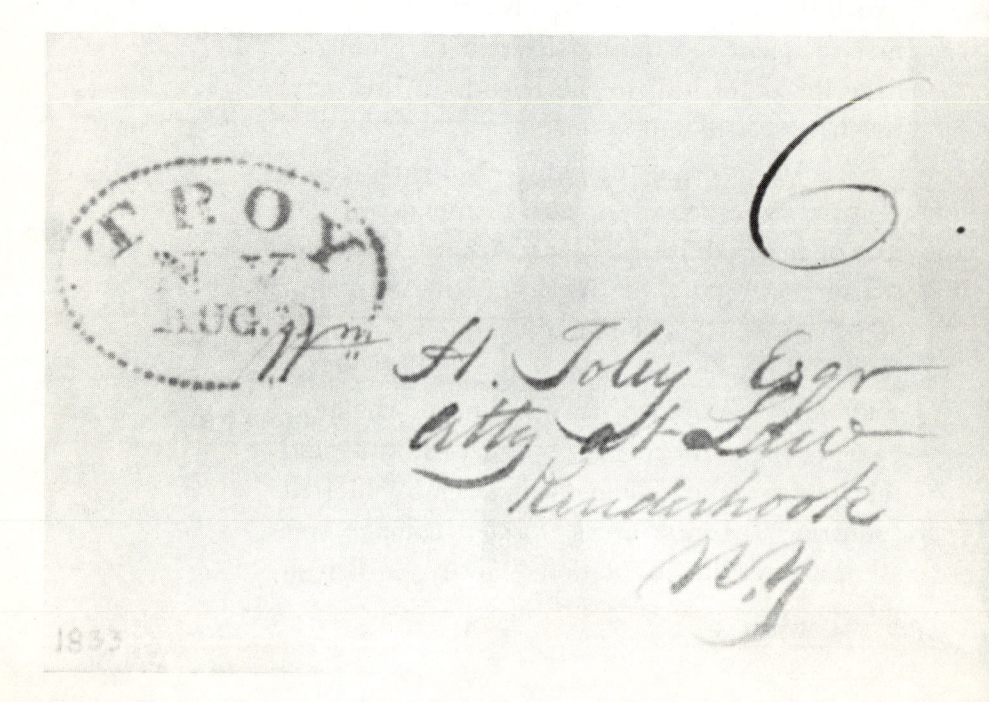

The letters were not prepaid. The mailing office wrote the amount of the postage required on the corner of the item, and the recipient was required to pay that amount on receipt. It was even considered a breach of courtesy to prepay an item of mail, because of the implication that the receiver was unable to afford the cost of his mail. The odd postage rates imposed during this period were, for each page, 6 cents up to 30 miles; 10 cents for from 30 to 80 miles; 80 to 150 miles was 12½ cents; 150 to 400 miles was 18 cents; and over 400 miles was 25 cents, or two-bits. The Spanish coin called a piece-of-eight had the equivalent value of $1.00. Divided into eight parts, each part, or bit, was worth 12½ cents. Often the coin itself was cut into eight wedge-shaped pieces, or bits. From this practice comes our slang word, two-bits, meaning a quarter dollar.

The letter shown here was mailed in 1833, from Troy, New York, to Kinderhook, New York. Such items are collected for their town markings, of which this is an excellent example; for the postal rates written on them; for the class of mail they represented; or for the names of important people to whom they were sent, as well as for the content of the message.

Section 9

TRANSPORTATION LEAFLETS

Paper Americana

As a part of transportation collecting, these leaflets are valued items. However, this particular kind is a bit different from the usual run of leaflets. Books were issued in those times containing pages advertising many different companies. They served much the same purpose as do our present-day yellow page directo-

BOSTON AND NEW YORK,

VIA NEWPORT AND FALL RIVER.

BAY STATE LINE.

This Route is by steamer from New York to Fall River, 180 miles, and thence by railroad, 53 miles, (one hour and forty minutes,) to Boston. On this route are the well-known steamers

EMPIRE STATE,	1650 tons burthen,	Capt.	Benjamin Brayton,
BAY STATE,	1600 " "	"	William Brown,
STATE OF MAINE,		"	Thomas Jewitt.

The Company is also building a new steamer, which will be the largest steamboat afloat. She will measure nearly 2200 tons,—length 345 feet,—breadth of beam, hull 45 feet and over guards 87 feet,—depth of hold 15 feet. She will have 112 state rooms, and sleeping accommodations for nearly twice the number that either the other boats can accommodate. She will be on the Line early in the summer.

These Boats are not surpassed, either in strength or safety, by any other boats ever constructed, and are elegantly and substantially fitted up with everything calculated to contribute to the ease, comfort and safety of travelers. One of them leaves New York every afternoon, (Sunday excepted,) at 5 o'clock P. M., (at 4 o'clock in the winter months,) and arrives at Fall River at an early hour in the morning, whence, after a comfortable night's rest, the traveler may proceed direct to Boston by steamboat train.

Passengers from Boston to New York take the steamboat train which leaves the Old Colony Railroad Depot, Boston, every afternoon, (Sundays excepted,) for Fall River, arriving at the latter place in time for an early supper on board one of the above boats, which starts for New York immediately on arrival of the train.

Providence passengers are forwarded to and from Fall River by steamers Bradford Durfee or Canonicus.

For all further particulars see bills and advertisements of the day.

Wm. BORDEN, Agent,
70 & 71 WEST STREET, NEW YORK.

ries of the telephone companies. Many collectors collect these pages and have them colored and framed. As a matter of fact, many artists specialize in just this kind of art form, creating paintings out of these leaflets suitable for framing as a collection of transportation items. Those leaflets having pictures of boats, trains, automobiles, streetcars, and other types of transport are in greater demand than those merely advertising the services.

Section 10
NEWSPAPERS

In recent years collecting pages of old newspapers—especially the front pages—has become popular. Many companies have been formed offering the service of sending reprint facsimiles of the front pages of your home town papers for your birthdate. The interest in this kind of collection is, of course, the news of the days of long ago, but even this category has been divided into the collection of papers from one city, one state—perhaps your home state, or one country.

Now, more than ever, old newspapers are becoming available at very low prices in

Paper Americana

25

The London Chronicle.

Vol. LXXXIII.   [369]   N° 6105.

From TUESDAY, APRIL 17, to THURSDAY, APRIL 19, 1798.

Wednesday, April 18.

From the LONDON GAZETTE of April 17.

Admiralty Office, April 16.

Copy of a Letter from Capt. Sir Henry Trollope, of his Majesty's Ship Russel, to Mr. Nepean, dated at Spithead, the 14th of April 1798.

SIR,

I BEG leave to acquaint you, that on the 11th ultimo, his Majesty's ship Jason, in company with the Russel, burnt a small French brig, in ballast, bound from Brest to Nantz; and on the 10th ultimo his Majesty's ships Russel and Jason captured the Bon Citoyen, a French brig privateer of 12 guns and 61 men, from Granville; had been out 14 days, and taken nothing. I have the honor to be, &c.
HENRY TROLLOPE.

War Office, April 17.

2d reg. of Dragoons. Peter Hay to be Cornet, by purchase, vice Ker, promoted.

6th ditto. Philip Glover to be Cornet, by purchase, vice Dearden, promoted.

12th reg. of Light Dragoons. Capt. Lord Blantyre, from the 31st foot, to be Captain, vice Barton, who retires.

29th ditto. Ensign Francis Halstead, from the 12th foot, to be Captain, without purchase, vice Gregory, promoted.

Coldstream reg. of Foot Guards. John Treadwell Simpson to be Assistant Surgeon, vice Thomas, who has resigned.

1st bat. of the 1st reg. of Foot. Ensign Sir John Gordon, Bart. to be Lieutenant, by purchase, vice Dunne, who retires.

16th reg. of Foot. Serjeant Major Henry Magill to be Adjutant, vice Davies, who resigns.

22d ditto. Lieut. James Scargill, from the half pay of the late 95th foot, to be Lieutenant, vice Pearse, who exchanges.

23d ditto. Serjeant Major Henry Harding to be Adjutant, vice Keith, appointed Paymaster.

31st ditto. Lieut. John Grosier, from the 80th foot, to be Captain, by purchase, vice Lord Blantyre, appointed to the 12th light dragoons. John Stafford to be Ensign, by purchase, vice Turner, promoted.

35th ditto. Cæsar Cokleugh Armett to be Ensign, by purchase, vice French, promoted in the 4th dragoon guards.

44th ditto. F. Ewin to be Ensign, by purchase, vice Henderson, promoted.

45th ditto. David Gregory to be Ensign, without purchase, vice Inglis, who resigns.

46th ditto. Capt. Lieut. Edward Sebright, from the 24th light dragoons, to be Captain, by purchase, vice Rainey, promoted in the 60th foot.

49th ditto. Ensign William Carr to be Lieutenant, by purchase, vice Hacau, promoted in the 67th foot.

51st ditto. Edward Stokes to be Ensign, by purchase, vice Lyle, promoted in the 66th foot.

58th ditto. Le Gendra Parkhurst to be Ensign, by purchase, vice Tolley, promoted in the 4th foot.

60th reg. of Foot.—To be Captains. Captains Ferd. Ernest De Gerardy, Ladislaus De Villers Maisburgh, Antony Auguste Baron D'Erp, and Lewis Schneider, all from Hompesch's chasseurs.—To be Lieutenants: Lieuts. Lewis Baron de Hesselrode Hagenport, John Antony Wolf, Peter Frederic Blasière, Frederic William B. De Gille, and — Rader, all from Hompesch's chasseurs. Lieut. Adolphus Munsthal, from Lowenstein's fuzileers.—To be Ensigns: Ensigns M. Ferd. Henckel, Charles William Henry Koch, George Henry Zuhlke, and George Philip Schuleder, all from Hompesch's chasseurs.

73d ditto. Ensign Charles Hanse, from the 19th foot, to be Lieutenant, by purchase, vice the Duke of Manchester, who retires.

88th ditto. Major Alexander Duff to be Lieutenant Colonel, by purchase, vice Sedli, who retires on the half-pay of Major. Major Francis John Wilder, from the half-pay of the late 106th foot, to be Major, vice Duff.

Queen's Rangers—Brevet Lieut. Col. David Shank to be Lieutenant Colonel Commandant, vice Major General Simcoe, appointed to the command of the 81st foot. Brevet Lieut. Col. Samuel Smith to be Major. Brevet Lieut. Col. Æneas Shaw to be Captain of a company, vice Shank. Capt. Lieut. William Mayne to be Captain of a company, vice Smith.

INVALIDS.—Lieut. James Hanton, from the invalids at Alderney, to be Lieutenant in Major West's independent company of invalids at Jersey, vice Sheridan, deceased. Ensign J. B. Hemmings, from the invalids at Guernsey, to be Ensign in Lieut. Col. Dixon's independent company of invalids at Plymouth, vice Bowers, promoted in the garrison battalion.

STAFF.—Capt. Nicolas Ramsay, of the 2d foot, to be Major of brigade to the forces. Lieut. Col. K. A. Howard, of the Coldstream guards, to be Major of brigade to the foot guards. William Tindale, Clerk, to be Chaplain of the Tower, vice Cowper, who has resigned.

Newfoundland Regiment of Fencible Infantry.—Major Thomas Skinner, from the Royal engineers, to be Colonel. Capt. Christopher Aldridge, from the Royal Nova Scotia regiment, to be Major.—To be Captains of companies: William Ilham Eppis, and Philip Van Cortlinett, Esqrs. Capt. John Hierlihy, from the half pay of the Royal Nova Scotia regiment. Capt. Thomas Trimlett, from the Royal Newfoundland volunteers. Capt. John Bulger, from ditto. Capt. James Macbraire, from ditto. David Darling, Esq. Capt. Elias Rowe, from the Royal Newfoundland volunteers.—To be Lieutenants: Thomas Pitts, William Bullock, Francois J. Lellever, Lieut. George Berton, from the Royal Newfoundland volunteers. Lieut. Monier Williams, from ditto. William Humfrey, George A. E. Skinner, George Ballard, Lieut. William Lilly, from the half pay of the late Newfoundland regiment, James Gotchings, Lieut. William Colborne, from the Royal Newfoundland volunteers.—To be Ensigns: John Le Breton, Fuller Weeks, Thomas G. W. Eastaff, Robert P. Skinner, Peter Delberky, John Hosier, David Duggan, Thomas Dwyer.—To be Chaplain: The Rev. John Harries.—To be Adjutant: David Darling, Esq.—To be Quarter Master: Tho. Pitts.—To be Assistant Surgeon: David Duggan.

Ayrshire Fencible Cavalry.—Patrick Howe to be Cornet, vice Maids, who resigns.

Perthshire Fencible Cavalry.—Major Alexander Muir Mackenzie to be Lieutenant Colonel, vice Graeme, who resigns. Capt. John Morris to be Major, vice Mackenzie. Capt. Lieut. James Hay to be Captain, vice Murray. Lieut. James Moray to be Captain Lieutenant, vice Hay. Cornet James Mackenzie Stewart to be Lieutenant, vice Moray.

1st Bat. of the Rutsby and Goldborgh Fencible Infantry.—Capt. James Sinclair, of the late 83d foot, to be Major, vice James Moody, who resigns. Ensign John Thomson, from the half pay of the 81st foot, to be Ensign, vice Benjamin Sinclair, promoted.

Bolserdale Gentlemen and Yeomanry.—Valentine Henry Wilmot to be Lieutenant, vice Edwards, promoted. Thomas May to be Cornet, vice Norris, promoted. Richard Kargett to be Cornet.

Loyal Strath Eden Troop of Gentlemen and Yeomanry.—George Cheape, Esq. to be Captain Commandant.

Boyne Volunteers—John Peel, Esq. to be Captain. Abraham Hoskins, jun. Esq. to be Captain. Thomas Worthington, Esq. to be Captain Lieutenant. William Osborne, jun. to be First Lieutenant. Charles Peele to be Second Lieutenant. John Spender, jun. to be Second Lieutenant.

Chatham Volunteers—Thomas Bentley, Esq. to be Captain. Edward Boys to be Lieutenant. Thomas Colchester to be Ensign.

[Price Sixpence.]

1st Bat. of the 2d Regiment of the Royal Edinburgh Volunteers—John Rae to be Surgeon, vice Hay, who resigns.

Norwich Volunteers—Capt. John Patteson to be Major Commandant. Thomas Watson to be Ensign, vice Day, who resigns.

Nottingham Volunteers—John Elliott, Esq. and James Hooley, Esq. to be Captains. William Taylor and John Nixon to be Lieutenants. Edward Bardsley and Henry Holdsworth to be Ensigns.

Prescot Volunteers—Joseph Jackson to be Surgeon.

Wantage Volunteers—Lieut. Oldfield Yate to be Captain, vice Wheeler, who resigns. Second Lieut. George Garrat to be First Lieutenant, vice Yate. —— Wartnan to be Second Lieutenant, vice Garrat.

ERRATUM in the Gazette of the 10th instant.

INVALIDS.—For "Lieut. Jeremiah Martin, from the 10th foot, to be Lieutenant in Major West's independent company of invalids in Jersey, vice Sheridan, deceased;" read, "Lieut. Jeremiah Martin, from the 10th foot, to be Lieutenant in Major Campbell's independent company of invalids at Alderney, vice Hanton, removed to Jersey."

MEMORANDUM.—The exchange between Ensigns Thomas Hutchings, of the 60th foot, and Robert Oliphant, of the 65th foot, as stated in the Gazette of the 27th of February last, has not taken place. Lieut. Frederick Greene, of the 45th foot, is superseded, having absented himself without leave from the transport in which he was embarked to join his regiment.

Commissions in the Provisional Cavalry of the County of Stafford, signed by the Lord Lieutenant.

Sir John Wrottesley, Bart. to be Lieutenant Colonel Commandant. Walter Haynes, Esq. to be Major. Thomas William Winter, Edward Grove, and W. H. Worthington, Esqrs. to be Captains. Tho. Patten, Esq. to be Captain Lieutenant. John Molineux, Wm. Hyatt, and Henry Crockett, to be Lieutenants.

Commissions in the Pembroke Militia, signed by the Lord Lieutenant.

Henry Mathias, Esq. to be Deputy Lieutenant; Abraham Leach to be Deputy Lieutenant; and John Philipps Adams, Esq. to be Deputy Lieutenant; all dated March 28, 1797. Joseph Adams, Esq. to be Deputy Lieutenant; dated Jan. 18, 1798. Dudley Achland, Esq. to be Deputy Lieutenant; dated March 21, 1798.

Commissions in the Supplementary Militia and Provisional Cavalry for the County Palatine of Chester, signed by the Lord Lieutenant.

Supplementary Militia.

William Mackay, Esq. to be Lieutenant; dated March 8, 1798. Joseph Golding to be Lieutenant; dated March 15, 1798. Edward Davies Davenport, Esq. to be Captain; dated April 2, 1798. Robert Wright to be Ensign; dated April 3, 1798.

Provisional Cavalry.

W. Congreve to be Lieutenant; dated April 3, 1798.

Commissions in the East York Supplementary Militia, signed by the Lord Lieutenant.

Thomas Courtney to be Lieutenant; dated Feb. 17, 1798. Martin Sayer to be Lieutenant; dated Feb. 25, 1798.

Commission in the Royal Surry Militia, signed by the Lord Lieutenant.

The Right Hon. William Lord Grantley to be Colonel; dated Jan. 10, 1798.

BANKRUPTS.

William Robins Tyndale, of Woodchester, Gloucestershire, grocer, to surrender May 4, 7, 17, at the London Inn and Talbot Tavern, Bristol. Attornies, Mr. Patrick Lewis, Inner Temple, London; or Mr. John Gillett, Bristol.

Edward Owen, of St. James's-street, Westminster, taylor, to surrender April 22, 28, May 29, at Guild-

old bookstores and collector-dealers. This supply is augmented by the vast files in public libraries being released to the public as the libraries convert to microfilm. The newspapers themselves are photographed, then sold to collectors or dealers who, in turn, offer them to collectors. The illustration shows the front page of the London *Chronicle* from the year 1798—a real oldie.

Section 11
COMMUNICATION ITEMS

Paper Americana

Telephone and telegraph items of the past century are very popular, and the demand is growing all the time. The illustration shows the actual telegraph key in use in the office of the American Telegraph Company at Waterford, New York, in the early 1800s.

The American Telegraph Company was the most prominent rival of the Western Union Company. American Telegraph lines were stretched from north to south, while the lines of the Western Union Telegraph Company traveled east and west. During the Civil War, these systems were split in half, and it became increasingly difficult to send messages to various places, since one company or another would not have a line running in that direction. Finally all lines were merged into the great complex, Western Union Company.

Also from Waterford, New York, comes this telephone receiver used in the home of Mr. S. C. Bush. There is heavy interest among collectors for artifacts of our early technology, and telephone artifacts occupy a prominent place in this interest. This particular receiver

Paper Americana

28

was the forerunner of our modern telephones, and was designed to be spoken into, then held against the ear to listen for the reply, serving the dual purpose of transmitter and receiver.

Paper Americana

Chapter two

Bag Labels

★★★★★★★★★★★★★★★★★★★★★★

Bag Labels

You name it—somebody collects it. If it isn't collected at the moment, it is perfectly simple to start the ball rolling. Once, when I was old enough to know better, I had a discussion with a couple of friends about the pack-rat instinct in animals (and human beings). I stated definitely, that, given any impetus at all, *any* person could be started on his way as a collector of trivia. My idea was poo-poohed, and we got into a heated argument about it. The upshot being that I said I would produce a collector within a month. Little did I realize what I was about to start.

For several days I scratched my head looking for the most useless thing I could think of. Finally, when accompanying my wife to the market, I hit upon the perfect thing. Each paper sack dished out by the clerk to hold the groceries had a label on one side. Printed in blue, black, or red ink, they stated the make and capacity of that size bag. Perfect. When I got home, I dug out all the old paper bags I could find, and cut the labels from them, taking care to cut them neatly square, and to smooth out any rumples in the paper. I took my hoard of perhaps fifty of the labels to work with me, and, every chance I got I would take them out of my pocket and pore over them in as surreptitious a manner as I could assume.

Each time someone would approach, I would hastily hide them, fumbling a bit so they could see what I had—all by accident, of course. Finally one poor innocent guy happened along. The conversation went something like this. "What are you hiding?"

"Oh, nothing. Nothing at all. Just some stuff I had in my pockets."

"Lemme see?"

"Nah. Nah, they're nothing to look at."

"Come on, let me see." Reaching for

Bag Labels

my wrist, he pulled my hand out of my pocket, still clutching the bundle of bag labels. Several fell to the floor—quite accidently, naturally, as I made a feeble effort to conceal them.

"What are these?" the fellow said as he picked them up and looked at them.

"Just old bag labels."

"Are they valuable?"

"No. No value at all. Just some old stuff I was keeping in my pocket."

"They must have some value, or you wouldn't save them."

"No. Unh-unh. They aren't worth anything. Junk."

"I don't believe you. They must be worth something. You just don't want anybody else to know about it, that's all." He stalked off in a huff. Fortunately one of the men I had had my discussion with was within eyesight and earshot of the little play, and witnessed it from beginning to end. He came over, his jaw swinging loosely. "I just don't believe it," he exclaimed. "That poor sap."

"Wait," I told him. "Just wait a couple of days."

Bag Labels

Sure enough, a few days later the man came over to my desk, carrying a shoe box which he opened triumphantly to display the contents. It was jam-packed with bag labels of all kinds and descriptions. "You aren't the only one," he exclaimed triumphantly. "I've got some too. You just wait. I'm going to get a bundle of these things before I'm through."

In less than a year that man's house was *littered* with boxes stuffed with bag labels.

A paper bag just wasn't safe anywhere in the entire city. He went from store to store, making small purchases in order to obtain bags. He would cadge them from the storekeepers, he would pull them out of garbage cans, and he became a regular hanger-on at the town dump. I don't know how many tens of thousands of bag labels he collected, but they certainly were countless.

Several years later, in a city many hundreds of miles from the first one, I met a man who took me proudly into his study to show me his collection—of what? You guessed it—bag labels. He had them neatly mounted in looseleaf albums, arranged by sizes, colors, makes, and whatever. He had thousands of different ones. Then came the payoff. He told me he was only one of a whole group of bag label collectors, but that his collection was the most valuable of all. "Why I've already refused fifteen hundred dollars for my collection," was his comment.

I give up.

Bag Labels

Chapter three

Cigar Bands

★★★★★★★★★★★★★★★★★★★★★★

*Cigar
Bands*

When I was a small boy cigar-band collecting was a very popular occupation, and I remember walking along the curb, looking for a discarded cigar butt still encircled with a band. To a ten-year-old boy, the handling of a soggy, much chewed lump of tobacco was not

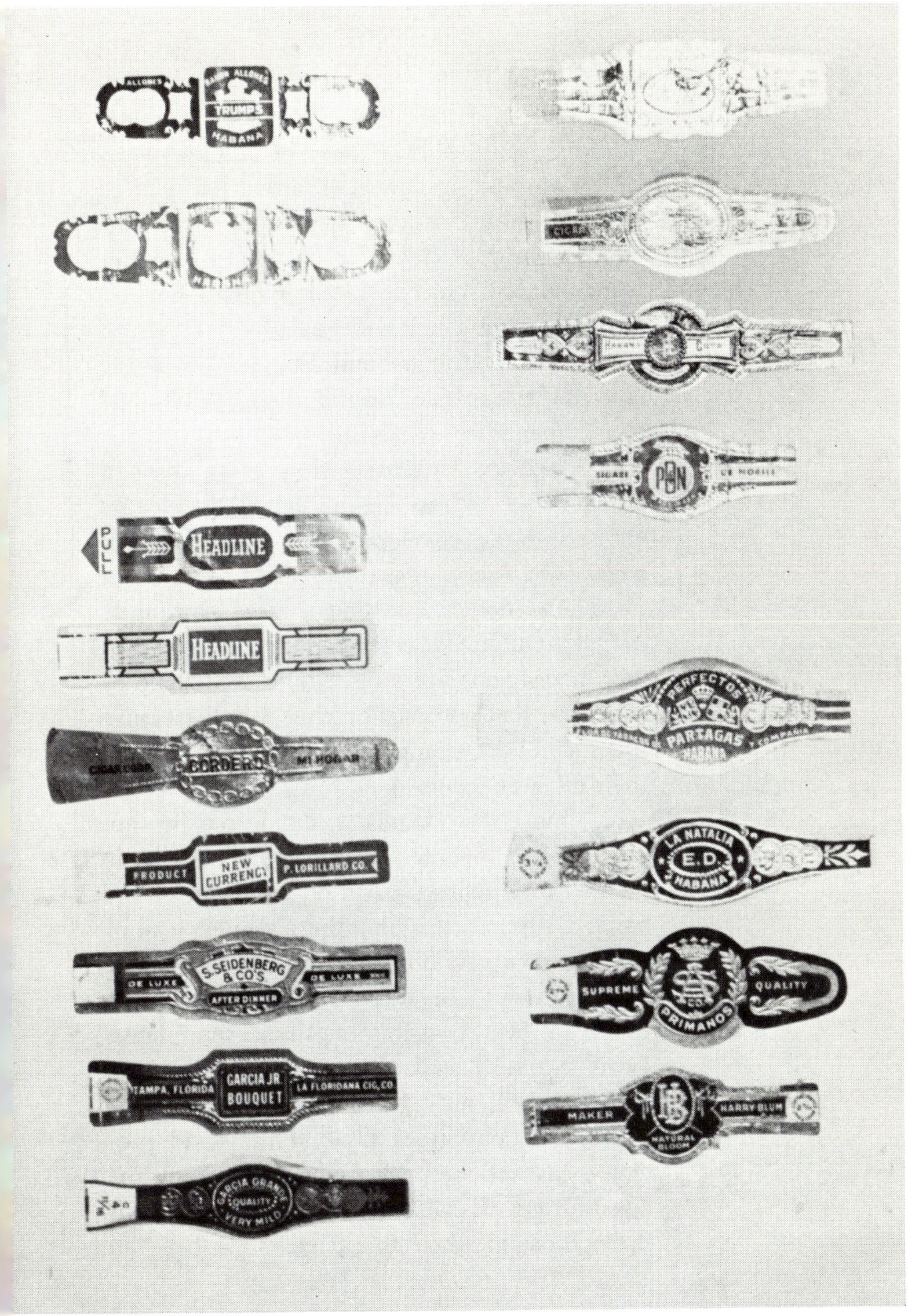
TRUMPS
HABANA
PULL
HEADLINE
HEADLINE
CIGAR CORP.
BORDERO
MI HOGAR
PRODUCT
NEW CURRENCY
P. LORILLARD CO.
DE LUXE
S. SEIDENBERG & CO'S
AFTER DINNER
TAMPA, FLORIDA
GARCIA JR. BOUQUET
LA FLORIDANA CIG. CO.
GARCIA GRANDE
QUALITY
VERY MILD
PERFECTOS
PARTAGAS
HABANA
Y COMPANIA
LA NATALIA
E.D.
HABANA
SUPREME
QUALITY
PRIMANOS
MAKER
HARRY BLUM
NATURAL BLOOM

at all as disgusting as it is in retrospect, but the thrill of finding a really rare and unusual cigar band still lingers in my memory.

A more sanitary way of adding to my collection was by hanging around a United Cigar store, and asking the customers for the bands from their cigars. I don't remember ever being refused. On one of his trips to Europe, my father returned with a large number of bands from Germany and France. I was the envy of the entire neighborhood, with real *foreign* bands in my album.

Not too long ago, while going through a bundle of old papers in the attic, I came across a large envelope filled with notebook pages. On examining them, imagine my surprise (and delight) to find a large portion of my old childhood cigar-band collection. Today these bands are long extinct, and some of them are real collector's items. I will treasure them as a part of my childhood, as well as for their intrinsic value.

Cigar Bands

Since the bands I discovered in my papers were mounted on pages by the simple method of a spot of paste on each end of the band, I suppose this was the accepted way of keeping them. At any rate it is a good way if they are not to be transferred at any time. I think, however, that in some future spare hour, I will carefully soak the bands off the pages and slip them into the transparent pockets of a postage stamp stock book. This would protect them and keep them intact without the possibility of damage to the ends of the bands through pasting them to a page.

Chapter four

Soap Wrappers

★★★★★★★★★★★★★★★★★★★★★

*Soap
Wrappers*

An interesting item that is collected by people who travel either for business or on vacation, is individual bars of soap. Many hotels, motels, and many restaurants use small bars of soap packaged especially for them. So each person has a fresh cake of soap that has not been used by anyone else. This is for sanitary reasons.

These small cakes are collected either for the name of the soap, or the place from which it was taken, or as mementos of a trip of some kind. The soap itself is not of as great importance to a collection as is the wrapper. Many collectors carefully undo the wrappers, ironing them out to lie flat so they can be mounted in a looseleaf book or an album of one kind or another. The soap is used, since the bar is of no interest to the collection.

Soap Wrappers

Some of the brands of soap found in these individual bars are many, many years old. Sweetheart soap was around when I was a small boy, as were Cashmere Bouquet, Ivory, and Palmolive, among many others. Today, if you listen to the television ads, you are not getting yourself clean if you use "soap," but only if you use some of the chemical combinations filled with all kinds of cleansers and detergents.

Chapter five

Automobile Plates
★★★★★★★★★★★★★★★★★★★★★★

*Automobile
Plates*

I met a man one day who told me that he had a collection of New York State automobile license plates, complete with a specimen from every year. Talking with him, I learned that the collecting of license plates is

39

a going thing, and there is keen interest among collectors to find plates in good condition. They are collected as a state item, as my friend did, with the collector attempting to get a specimen of every single year; or as a country-wide collection, having a plate from every state in the union, or even better, a world-wide collection, with samples from all countries issuing automobile plates.

A few years ago my wife and I took a vacation trip from one end of Canada to the other, then back through the United States. When in our travels we arrived at the extreme western part of Canada, I remembered seeing an automobile with a striking plate in the form of a polar bear. The flash I got of it as the car sped by just enabled me to make out the word "territory" but I could not read the rest. A little deduction led me to believe that the plate was issued by the Northwest Territories in Canada, and, for this book, I set about trying to locate one of those plates.

Automobile Plates

I wrote letters all over, but had no success until finally I had a reply from the Chamber of Commerce in British Columbia, telling me that they had forwarded my letter to the Government of the Northwest Territories. Then I had three more letters in quick succession—two of them from Travelarctic, the Division of Tourism of the Northwest Territories, and the third from the government offices of the Territories. The government letter gave a list of different years and different kinds of automobile, truck, and motorcycle plates, from the year 1964 to the present. A collector can purchase any of them for a certified check or money order in the amount of $5.00 made payable to the Government of the Northwest Territories, P. O. Box 1320, Yellowknife, N.W.T. These plates will bear the numbers 000, or any other number the collector wishes to show on his plate.

41

The letters from the division of tourism told me that plates were available from the Registrar of Vehicles, at the government address I've already given you. The last letter stated that used plates were sold for $2.50 each at Sutherland's Drugs Ltd., P. O. Box 670, Yellowknife, N.W.T., XOE IHO., and also were sold by Roy's Confectionery, P. O. Box 938, Yellowknife, N.W.T., XOE IHO.

Automobile Plates

Chapter six

Bottles

★★★★★★★★★★★★★★★★★★★★★

Bottles

Collecting old bottles has become almost a business today. For a long time it was just a hobby for people who liked to walk in the woods and would pick up an old glass bottle when they would see one. Now, however, there are several books published on the subject of old bottle identification and prices, and some of the bottles are hundreds of dollars each if you buy them from dealers or other collectors.

The old-fashioned Ball and Mason jars that grandmother used to use for canning fruits and vegetables are also collected, and some of the older styles are very rare, indeed. They were made out of a kind of glass that, under prolonged exposure to the sun, turned violet in color. These colored specimens have an even greater value than do the plain clear kind.

In olden times bottles were mostly hand made. They were irregular in size and shape, and the glass used was usually full of tiny bubbles. Then the makers of bottles began to blow them inside of molds to make more uniform shapes and sizes. The molds were in parts so they could be separated to remove the bottle when the glass had hardened. These molds were in two parts, three parts, or more, and they left lines in the glass by which the type of mold could be identified. It was a short step from there to put writing in the molds which would be impressed on the bottle, either as raised lettering, or indented, depending on whether the lettering was raised in the mold or depressed.

The stoppers were usually simple corks, but many manufacturers of bottles tried very ingenious ways of stoppering their bottles, some of them being very complicated. One of the latter methods was to mold a marble or ball of glass or porcelain inside the neck of the bottle when it was being made. If carbonated

Bottles

liquids were put into the bottle, the pressure of the gas generated would keep the marble pressed tightly up at the top of the neck, sealing it off. A push down on the marble would release the pressure so you could pour the fluid out.

Porcelain stoppers, circled with a rubber washer and fastened to the neck of the bottle with heavy wire, was a common method of stoppering. These were in use before the invention of the crown metal cap, and I can remember my parents (with my inexpert help) making homemade rootbeer and storing it in such stoppered bottles.

Bottles are where you find them. The great majority of them are buried in woods, farmlands, and fields. Sometimes one will come across a dumping site where bottles may abound. The old ones are usually deep under the rest of the trash, and you may have to sort over a lot of material before you begin to unearth the bottles.

After they are found, bottles have to be cleaned. They often fill up with soil, lying on their sides year after year, with seasonal rains and snows sifting the debris into them until they are plugged tightly. Some soils, containing large amounts of minerals, stain the glass —often so badly that the stain cannot be removed entirely.

As one bottle authority explains—bottle collecting is a summer hobby, and a reason for taking many pleasant hikes and walks through the fields and woods. Wintertime is the time of cleaning and classifying, when evenings too bad to enjoy outside can be spent in dissolving the dirt out of the treasures, and attempting to remove the stains.

Stains are removed by washing, using bleach, drain-cleaning chemicals, or acids. Such things can be dangerous to use by younger people and great care should be taken. Adult supervision is desirable when the summer's accumulation of bottles is cleaned. Good ventilation must be provided when using such things as acids or bleach. Some drain chemicals like Drano will generate gas which can be very harmful if used in confined quarters and inhaled.

Steel wool or sandpaper should never be used to clean a bottle, since much of the value is a surface free from scratches, and the glass from which old bottles were made was very soft and easily scored with abrasive materials.

Bottles having any kind of stopping device are worth more in a collection when the stopper is intact. It does not necessarily have to work perfectly, but it should be on the bottle with all its parts.

Unscrupulous dealers in old things will often take a valuable bottle and coat it with lacquer or one of the epoxies. This will effectively hide all scratches and make the bottle look as though it just came out of the factory. Beware of such fakes. The surface of the bottle will feel smooth and greasy if it has been so treated, and if the material used was lacquer, it can be scratched with the fingernail.

Bottles

Chips, especially around the lip of the opening, also detract both from the appearance and the value of a specimen. Those bottles which over a long period of time were exposed to the rays of the sun and turned violet, or, as a bottle collector calls it, amethyst, in color, are especially valuable. Since a bottle exposed to strong ultraviolet light will turn the same color, there has been a lot of counterfeiting of amethyst bottles lately. The only way to be sure that you have a truly naturally colored bottle is to dig it up yourself.

One bottle authority's method of grading bottles is as follows. **POOR**: Badly stained, scratched, or eroded. Chipped or cracked. Broken but with missing piece. **GOOD**: Mineral stain or rust inside bottle. Small chips missing, and some scratching. **FINE**: Slight mineral stains, no oxidation on glass, chip marks, but no chips actually taken out, no cracks, and not excessively scratched. **VERY FINE**: Just a hint of mineral staining on inside. A very few slight scratches, no chips or chip marks. **PERFECT**: Like new. Stopper present and working, if a stoppered bottle. (Corks are not counted as stoppers, although sometimes they can be present also.)

Bottles

Chapter seven

Insulators
★★★★★★★★★★★★★★★★★★★★★

Insulators

When the first railroads were built across this land, the telegraph wires accompanied the tracks. The first wires strung were single strands of iron wire, fastened to whatever sup-

48

port was available, with poles set in between where needed. Thus came into being the first need for electrical insulators, and thus was born the hobby of insulator collecting.

As the wire stringing crews worked along the track right-of-way, they would erect the poles in a line, then climb up them, fasten the insulator in place, and secure the wire strand to the insulator. If, while performing these tasks they dropped one of the glass or porcelain insulators, heaven forbid that they would climb down the pole to retrieve it, climbing back up again to secure it. No, they just let it lie where it fell and put on another insulator. If they remembered it, after they climbed down the pole to go to the next one, they picked up the dropped insulator. More often, they left it in the weeds and prairie grass, slowly to become buried by the seasonal action of the weather.

Sometimes as fast as the wire was strung along a track, the Indians of the plains would tear it down. Many tribes believed that the white man's devil lived in the humming wire, and were afraid to touch it. Others thought the same thing, but were brave enough to attempt to destroy this evil monster, and, when tearing down the wire, they would retrieve the insulator as a part of the white man's evil gods and take it to their lodge or camp, where it would be cherished as a captive god of the enemy. War dances would be held around this object when they were getting ready to start out to defend their lands and lives against the encroaching whites.

Insulators

So, the Indians were actually the first insulator collectors. Today their hated enemy is running all over the country searching for specimens of these artifacts, but for an entirely different reason. The scarcity of supply versus the demand for the product. Some insulators have a value of $1500.00! Most of them go for a dime to a half-dollar. It is far more fun to hunt for your own, and these are free.

An excellent way to hunt for insulators is to take a three-pronged garden cultivator with you when you go on your next vacation trip. Then, when you drive along the highway paralleling a stretch of railroad track, get out of the car and walk along the track. You can walk the track, stopping to rake around at the bottom of each pole. Chances are you won't find anything, but then again, you might.

The more wild the country, the better chance you have of finding a very old insulator. The very best places are in the mountain country where homes, towns, and cities are few and far between.

It is a real thrill to strike a perfect specimen of old, old, glass buried a few inches beneath the ancient crossarm or an old telegraph pole in a secluded and forgotten area of the country. All sorts of visions of yelling railroad crews, swearing wire crews, and howling Indians can trip through your thoughts as you pick it up and brush the dirt from the surface.

The oldest kinds of insulators were just glass blobs with a ridge around their middle to which the wire could be tied, and a socket

Insulators

inside so the insulator could be jammed down onto a wooden peg on the pole. Later ones were threaded inside the socket with coarse threads corresponding to threads on the wooden pegs. This method of fastening them to the pegs was far more secure than just jamming them down. The threading of the sockets has continued to the present day, and now we are making insulators of many, many kinds—not just the simple thimble-shaped ones used along railroad tracks.

Insulators

Chapter eight

Keys

★★★★★★★★★★★★★★★★★★★★★★

Keys

Keys are another popular collectible item, and some of the old keys are really interesting. In ancient times locks were simple devices, and, as a result, the keys were simple, too.

That is, they did not have to turn many tumblers in the lock, so the levers were either plain, or with one or two grooves to fit the particular lock it was made for.

Many of the old-time keys were enormous compared with those of modern times, and jail keys were about the largest of all. The poor jailer had a real burden to carry around, the keys being a foot or more in length and weighing a pound or two. Old dungeon keys in the castles of Europe were also huge and weighty.

Most of the ancient locks were locks only because of the shape of the keyhole. By this I mean that anything that would enter the keyhole would unlock the lock mechanism, so the keyholes were made in all kinds of fancy shapes, and the keys to fit them. After the key entered the keyhole, all it had to do was turn one or two tumblers to release the lock. It was the fact that the person wishing to open the lock did not have an implement shaped to enter the keyhole that made the device safe from intrusion. Today this would not keep a thief out for more than a moment or two.

As fast as locks were designed to be "burglar-proof," men learned to pick them open. There really is no such thing as a pick-proof lock. Some of the extremely complicated locks would take a long time to open without the proper key, but do not doubt that it can be done by some clever person or another. The axiom that locks are for honest people, is only too true.

Keys

The evolution of keys can be followed by looking at the lever ends of the older ones. Slowly they become more and more intricate in design, until they reach a limit of possibility of change. Then the locks were changed to different systems, permitting an entirely new class of key to be made for them. These, too, became more and more intricate in design, until once again the locks underwent a renovation.

When keys operating from inside only had exhausted their design possibilities, the locks were made to be operated from both sides of the key simultaneously. This opened a new avenue of combinations that were heretofore impossible with one-sided keys. When

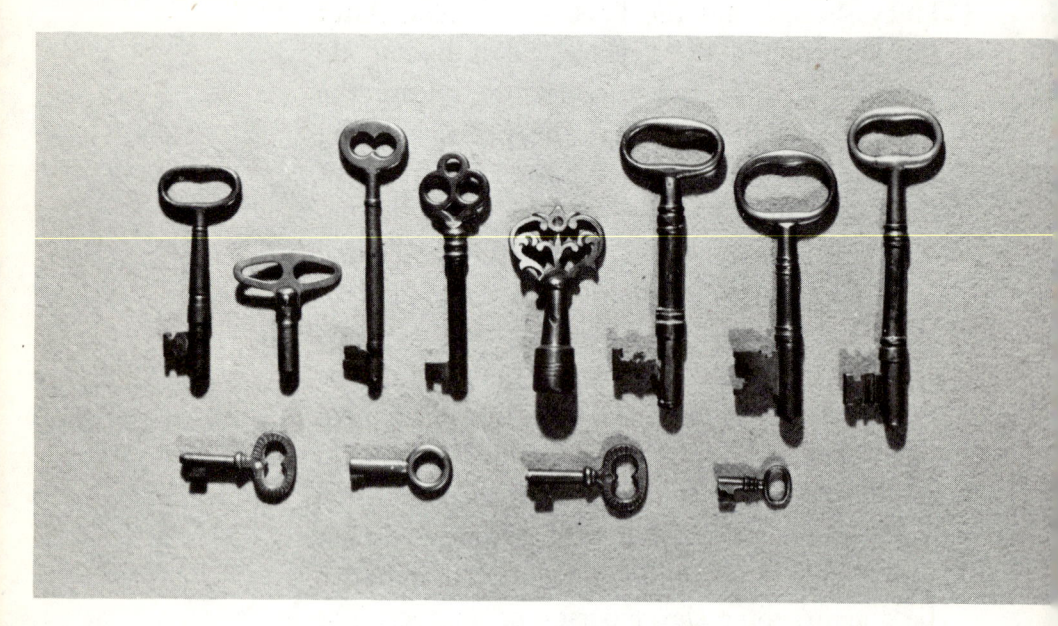

both sides reached their limit of complication, a new design in locks came forth.

So the design of locks and the companion design of their keys continues to advance. Eventually mankind will have to resort to an entirely new system of keeping its valuables safe from each other. The logical conclusion will be locks operating electronically, keyed by the fingerprint of the owner, but here, too, clever thieves can circumvent the safeguard, by engraving counterfeit fingerprints to press against the activating cell. Maybe retinal patterns will be the answer to the truly pick-proof lock. You merely hold your eyeball up against an aperture so a photocell can read the pattern of your retina, and the door will magically open in your face. Some fun.

Keys

Chapter nine

Match Book Covers
★★★★★★★★★★★★★★★★★★★★★★★

*Match Book
 Covers*

This is not a new hobby. It has been a popular occupation since the first matches were put up in books. There were several reasons for the development of book matches. One was the convenience of carrying them around. Un-

HI-HO MOTEL
HILLYARD MOTEL
CRUDELE'S RESTAURANT
CANDY CANE MOTEL
SCOTT SHADY COURT
NEVADA HOTEL
hick'ry pit
DUTCH RATHSKELLER
HICKORY HOUSE
Shanghai Inn
GWYNN'S
Q. Lung
CROSSROADS MOTEL
ROMANO'S RESTAURANT AND BAR
COLONIAL MOTEL
ENGLISH MOTEL
CANDY CANE MOTEL
SCOTT SHADY COURT
2440 GRAND
in legendary
LARAMIE
wonderful
WYOMING
AL & DICK
STEAK HOUSE
BONANZA
SIRLOIN PIT
POE
LODGE No. 385
KINGS ROW
The NEVELE
Country Club
Coors

til the advent of the book match, people were forced to lug either a box of matches or to keep a number of loose matches in a pocket. This had several disadvantages.

At that time, safety matches were not in general use, and the matches of the day were the old-fashioned "sulphur" matches. This merely meant that the head was composed mainly of sulphur, and they could be ignited by rubbing them against almost anything. Sometimes they rubbed against each other in a pocket, setting some poor unfortunate on fire from the inside out, as it were.

The first safety matches were smaller than the "lucifers," as they were popularly called, but still made of wooden splints, and they were sold in small wooden boxes. Each side of the box carried a strip of the striking, or rather, igniting material.

Safety matches were safe by virtue of the fact that the ingredients making the match were simply divided into two parts. One part was placed on the head of the match, as usual. The other part was placed in the striking strip on the box. In order to ignite the match, the two parts had to be brought together with friction. In this way, the matches could not be ignited accidently, either in a pocket, or in the home, or by being chewed by a mouse. They were also considerably safer in the hands of small children, who only by accident would rub the head of the match on the striking strip of the box.

From the boxed safety match, it was

Match Book Covers

only a short step to the book match. The first of these were made of flat strips of wood stamped partially to split them, and, scored to make a line at which point the match could be snapped out of the pack. The book cover was made of thin cardboard, and the striking strip painted on the bottom of the front of the cover.

In the hands of a careless person, it was found that often the struck match would be slid up to the heads of the book igniting the entire pack in the palm of his hand. Severe burns would result from this practice, and so the striking strip is often placed on the back of the book cover instead of the front. A kind of safety, safety match. However, most of the book matches today still place the striking strip on the front, depending on the user to use his head as well as the match, and close the book before striking up.

As soon as book matches were invented, enterprising persons saw the great advantage of the little covers as a medium for advertising their wares. Each year, literally tens of millions of book matches are made with different advertising printed on the covers. This immediately creates a collecting item, and book match cover collecting has an extremely large following. As a matter of fact, albums are now manufactured in which the collector can safely keep his collection free from damage.

The method of collecting these items is carefully to remove the staple holding the book together, and take out the matches. The book

Match Book Covers

cover is then flattened out, ready for mounting in whatever way you wish to keep your collection.

Book match covers are collected in several different categories. Topical collections—such as books from motels or hotels; from restaurants; from places of amusement; from banks; or from any other kind of place. Covers from different states or different cities are a popular category. A cover from every place you stop on your vacation trip is still another way of collecting them. Then they are collected for the pictures on them. There are covers showing flowers, or girls, or scenes, or animals, or birds—the categories are numberless.

Match Book Covers

Chapter ten

Sugar Wrappers

★★★★★★★★★★★★★★★★★★★★★★★★

Sugar Wrappers

The wrappers used to package individual servings of sugar are in great demand, and clubs are being formed by persons who collect them. Two varieties of wrappers are usually used—those decorative envelopes which contain one level teaspoonful of granulated sugar, and the wrapper used to cover one sugar cube.

The White Ace company has issued an album with pages printed to accept the cube wrappers, and, if they are not opened flat, these will also hold the envelope style. However, since much information is usually printed on the back sides of the envelopes, I think it is better to keep them opened fully rather than intact.

The crimped edges of the envelopes should be trimmed away with scissors, and the sugar emptied out. The wrapper may then be opened and flattened for mounting in your album. Wrappers—especially the envelope kind—are printed in a kaleidoscope of colors, and a myriad of designs and motifs. There are, as in other collectible items, many different categories in which you might specialize. Birds, ships, automobiles, flowers or fruit, buildings, scenes—you name it, and there is probably a sugar wrapper with that design on it in use somewhere.

Sugar Wrappers

The condition of the wrapper is important, as is the condition of every single item that anyone collects. One that has been torn open or ripped is of far less interest than one that was carefully removed or opened.

Sugar wrapping collecting is an inexpensive hobby. In fact, free, since the servings of sugar are provided in almost every restaurant, hotel, motel and soda fountain, as well as in other places. Your vacation trip can be pleasantly recalled by looking over your collection of sugar wrappers from many of the places you stayed and ate during the trip.

Some of the envelope-type wrappers are not only beautiful, but they are informative as well. One large series had been put out bearing different pictures of wildlife, with a descriptive and informative paragraph on the back, along with an advertisement for the National Wildlife Foundation. Another beautiful series is of historical ships, and the backs of these wrappers contain information about the building of the ship illustrated on the other side. Still a third series in my collection bears printed admonitions concerning driving safety —something of use to most people behind the wheel of an automobile these days. I also have the part of a series showing the individual coats-of-arms of the provinces of Canada.

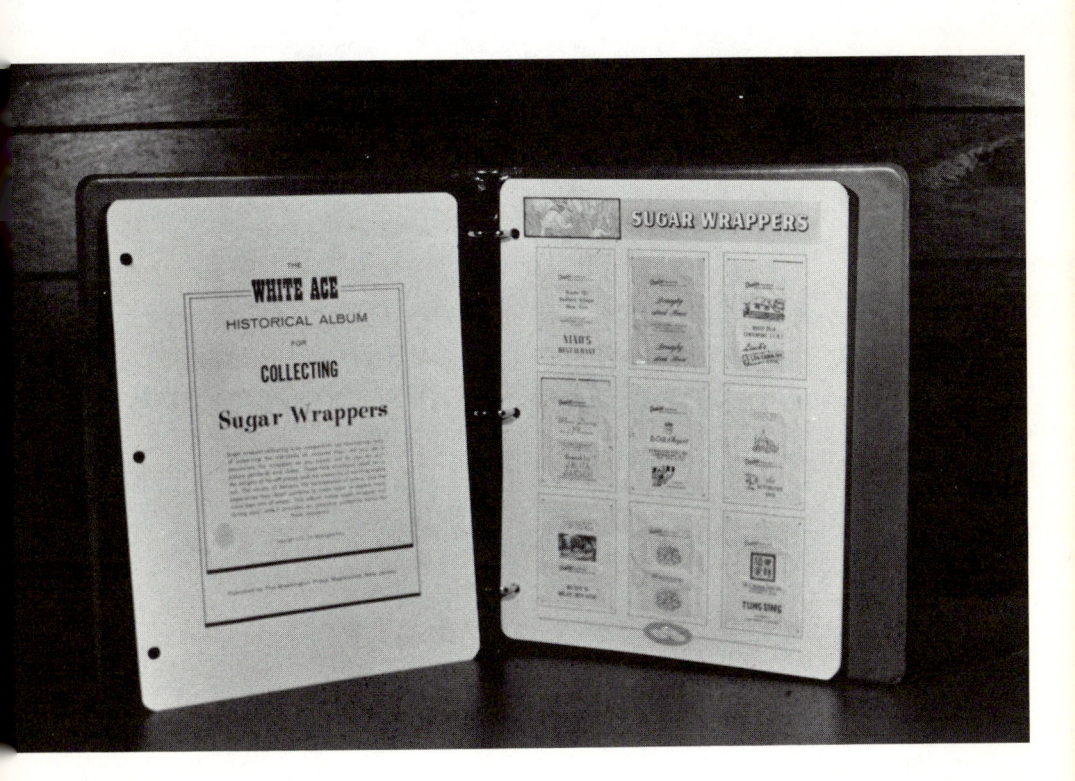

Birds and scenic locations throughout the country seem to be the two most often printed categories in the envelope wrappers. The sugar cube wrappers are much less colorful and interesting because of their smaller size. They are not nearly large enough to carry a scene or a drawing, so usually the markings on cube wrappers are the names of the places using them. Here, then, the possible categories are far fewer than those of the envelopes. You could specialize in wrappers from inns only, or motels only, or only hotels. You could build a collection of wrappers from cities, or states, or countries—Europe uses sugar, too, you know.

Sugar Wrappers

Chapter eleven

Buttons

★★★★★★★★★★★★★★★★★★★★★

"Button, button, who's got the button?" This somewhat ungrammatical query used to be the beginning of a child's game, but now it takes on a different meaning. Button collecting is a hobby that has been in vogue for many

decades. I had never seen a real collection of them until a few years ago when I happened to mention buttons to a friend. "Oh, my mother has been collecting buttons since she was a little girl." The friend took me over to her mother's house.

The mother who had collected since she was a little girl was then ninety years old! Spry as a chipmunk, she was delighted to show me her button collection. She had over *ten thousand* buttons, sewed on shirt cardboards, about 14″ by 18″ in size. Box after box of these cards were pulled from under beds, out of drawers, and from closet shelves. I didn't know there were that many buttons in the world!

Uniform buttons, dress buttons, shoe buttons (a species now long extinct), coat buttons, shirt buttons, buttons for which I could not estimate a use. Buttons made of metal, bone, plastic, pearl shell, wood, leather, almost any kind of material you could imagine, were represented in that unbelievable collection.

Buttons

The history of buttons goes back many centuries. Fasteners for clothing are necessities, and, when simple ties consisting of a sash or cord tied around one's waist were no longer enough, fasteners began to be used. The first ones were probably crude—perhaps a short twig or bone stuck through the fold of fabric like a pin. The American Indians used porcupine quills in this fashion to fasten their deerskin shirts and skirts. Large seeds, small pebbles, almost anything that could be attached to a garment has served in one fashion or an-

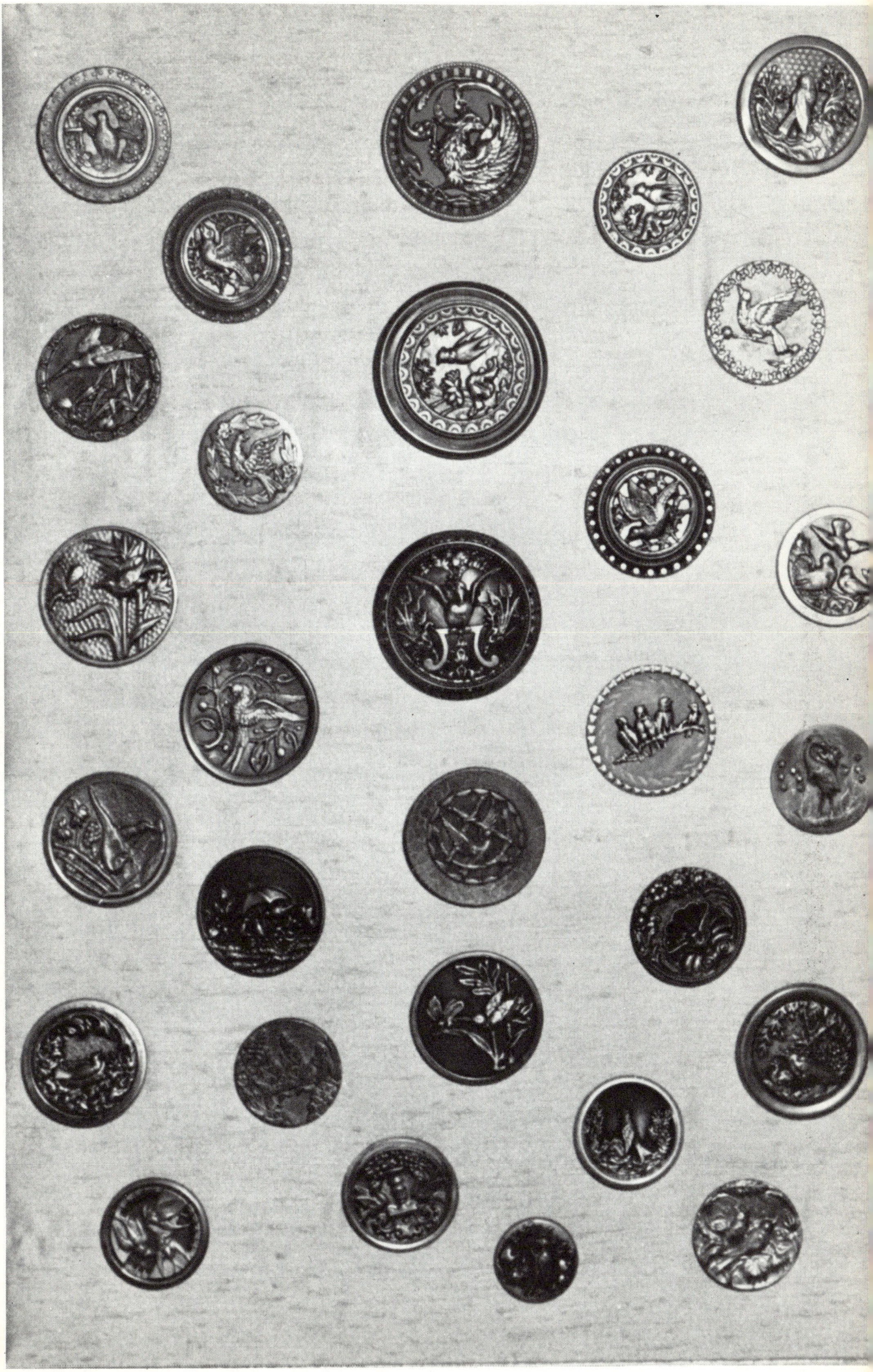

other to close a shirt or dress. Buttons as we know them were developed in the thirteenth and fourteenth centuries.

Buttons used by royalty were—and perhaps still are—made of gold, silver, and precious stones. Gem cutting is one of my hobbies, and I have myself made buttons for my wife and for friends out of gem stones set in silver. Each button is an individual piece of jewelry, and, of course, they are removed from the garment when it is discarded. So they can be used over and over on newer things to wear.

Old clothes, stored away in some attic and forgotten for many years, are good sources of old buttons. Rummage sales, where a garment may be purchased for a dime or a quarter, are another good source, since, usually those old things came out of someone else's attic. Garage sales, yard sales, and church bazaars are all good places to look for the old fasteners.

Buttons

Chapter twelve

Posters

★★★★★★★★★★★★★★★★★★★★★★★

In the days gone by, posters were a very popular method of advertising one thing or another. Some of them were merely notices of some kind of event—a concert, perhaps, or a fair.

The posters were pasted or tacked to walls of buildings, fences, telegraph poles, or any other support, and after posting, were left to disintegrate in the weather, or stay until someone took them down.

Posters can still be found attached to the walls of ancient barns, on covered bridges, on old buildings long since abandoned, as well as in attics and cellars. Some of them are in quite good condition, considering that the things they have been through—rain, sun, wind, and small boys—have contributed equally to the demise of many old and interesting posters.

Reproductions of some of these old advertising sheets are made by several companies, and they are often given away for coupons found on candy bars and other commodities, such as breakfast cereals. Naturally, a real poster collector would look down his nose at these imitations, but they still are a very good way to start a poster collection, and to become acquainted with the often beautiful representations depicted on them.

Poster collecting affords a cross section of the industries of the times. Companies vied with one another to put out the most colorful posters, in an attempt to catch the eye of the passer-by. As a usual thing, the poster collector does not have a large collection containing a great many specimens. There are not that many available. When a really good item is found, the poster makes an ideal decoration for the wall of the den, bedroom, or living room. They become a conversation piece in the home, and, if you can discover the story of the company printing them, it adds to the interest and value of the poster.

Posters

Chapter thirteen

Picture Post Cards

★★★★★★★★★★★★★★★★★★★★★

*Picture
Post Cards*

Post card collecting had been a hobby for a very long time. My grandmother used to collect cards when she was small, and kept up her hobby throughout her entire life. She died when she was ninety-six years old!

71

Picture Post Cards

Collecting became nearly a craze in the early 1900s. Some of the patterns of these cards were little short of outlandish. They were manufactured of a variety of materials, from straw matting, fabrics, leather, metal, and paper. Plastics were not yet developed, or there would certainly have been cards made from them. As a matter of fact, some modern post cards *are* made of plastic, and they even show their scenes in three dimensions.

The craze has died down considerably these days, but picture post card collecting is still very much a going thing, and in every city and town in the country one will find racks of dozens of colorful scenes, mostly showing places or things pertaining to that locality.

A card or two from every town you pass through will make a collection which will bring the trip back to mind every time you look at it. They can be kept in a file drawer, but a better way is to mount them with mounting corners in a post card album made for the purpose.

Oddly shaped post cards can be slipped into a clear plastic envelope first, and the envelope mounted with the corners in the album. These transparent envelopes may be bought from stamp dealers and hobby stores. Most department stores have a stamp and coin department which sells such envelopes, too.

Post cards are collected for the pictures on them, or perhaps only cards which have been sent through the mail. Other collectors save cards from different cities, states, or countries. When they are collected for their pictures, they are sometimes collected as specialty items—that is, cards showing only scenes, or animals, or birds, etc. There are many categories possible in collecting picture post cards. A collection of cards showing waterfalls is an interesting one, for example.

Some post cards are so unusual that you would never think of them going through the mail, but they did, and we can find these whacky post cards in old trunks, boxed and enveloped, forgotten in attics and cellars, or they can be purchased from dealers who root out these finds for their customers. Post cards are cheap enough if you buy them, most of them selling for a few cents each, but it is a lot more fun to find your own whenever possible.

Picture post cards may be collected in any of several different ways. They could show scenes from every place you went on a vacation trip. They could be collected of scenes all around your home town. They could be collected from every state in the country, or from every city in the state. They could also be the subjects of topical collections, such as cards showing only buildings, or only scenes of nature, or only animals, birds, ships, cars, almost any category you can think of.

A great many of the old-time picture post cards were photographic prints, rather than examples of printing or typesetting. For nearly a decade, there was a huge fad in collecting what were called "comic" post cards.

Picture Post Cards

These were usually weird or bizarre in the extreme. Maudlin rhymes were also a very popular theme.

As with any kind of collection, post cards should be in as nearly perfect condition as possible. If you have a folded or torn specimen, by all means keep it in your collection, but be on the lookout for a new post card to replace the damaged one, which then can be used for trading.

Picture
Post Cards

Chapter fourteen

Campaign Buttons

★★★★★★★★★★★★★★★★★★★★

Campaign Buttons

Several decades ago some political campaign manager got the bright idea of using large pin-type buttons as a means of getting the name of his candidate before the public eye. Thus, campaign buttons came into being,

75

and they are still with us. Each election brings forth buttons carrying a slogan or phrase for the candidate, and, often, a picture of the person as well.

Collecting these buttons has become a popular hobby, and there is active trading, buying, and selling going on among those enthusiasts. As a matter of fact, some of the very old campaign buttons have become so rare and valuable that they are now offered as reprints, the newly manufactured buttons being exact reproductions of the original ones. The only ways they can be told from the real thing is by the manufacturer's name printed on them, or by the word, "reproduction" printed on the inside edge of the button, or by their obvious newness.

As a general rule, the old buttons were made of tin, with a steel or brass pin snapped inside of them with which to attach the slogan to your lapel. The pictures themselves were printed on celluloid which was shrunk over the metal button base. The new reproductions are printed directly on the metal button. They came in many sizes, some of them nearly as large as saucers.

Campaign Buttons

Campaign button collecting presents a cross section of the political activity of the country, and, if you really want to make a striking display, you can research a short biography of each person represented, neatly typing this on a small card which can then be mounted under each button.

A piece of heavy cardboard covered with fabric of some kind will make a good

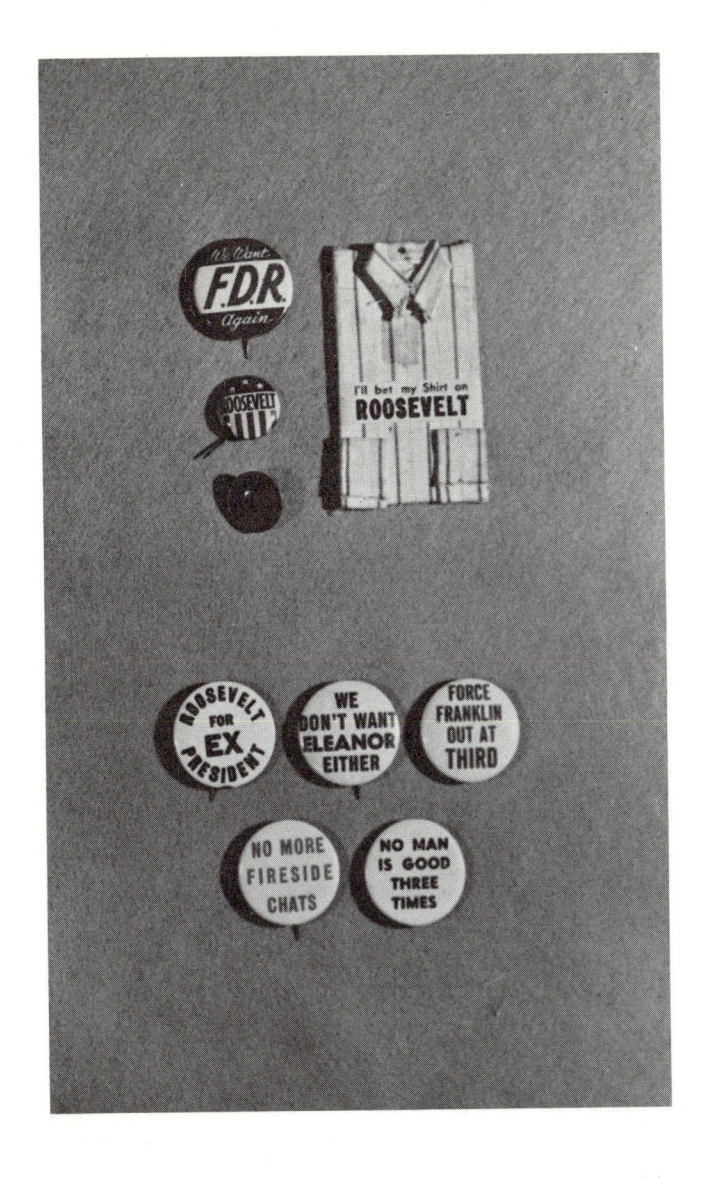

Campaign Buttons

mounting board for your collection, and this can be framed as a perfect wall decoration.

They may be collected topically if desired—buttons from Democrats or those from Republicans, specimens from both parties, presidential candidates only, or just anyone using campaign buttons in a general collection.

77

Chapter fifteen

Barbed Wire
★★★★★★★★★★★★★★★★★★★★★★

Barbed Wire

A few years ago my wife and I took an extensive automobile trip all through Canada and the United States. In the West we visited a great number of rock shops, collecting minerals for gem cutting. In most of those shops

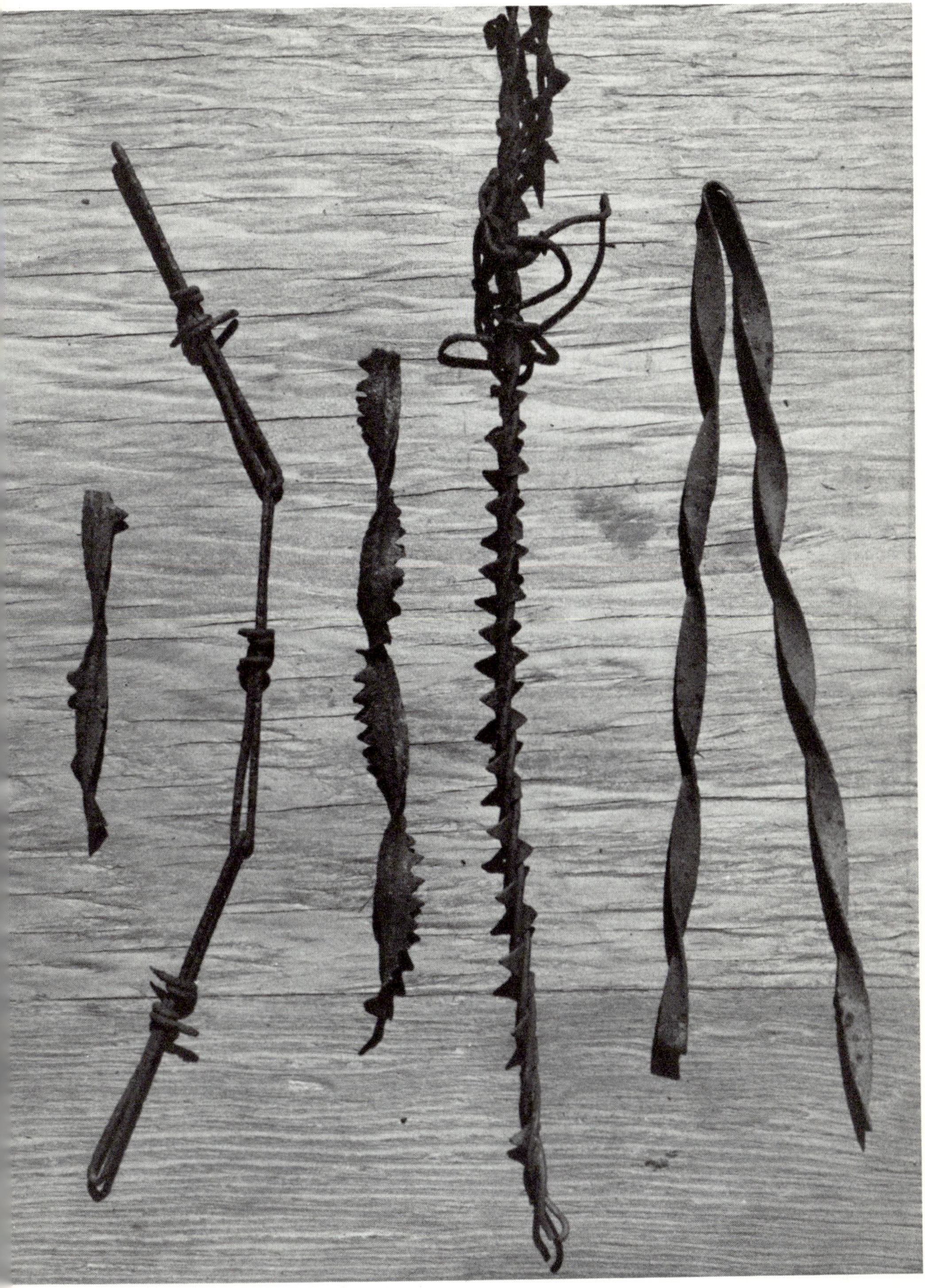

we saw bunches of short lengths of barbed wire for sale at a few cents per length. We didn't buy any. Who would want them? We forgot the human race of pack rats. Sure enough, when later I began researching collectible items, I found that antique barbed wire is a popular collectible.

Hundreds of different kinds of barbed wire have been invented and the designs of many of them have actually been patented so they could not be manufactured by other companies. Some of the styles are fantastic. Every method conceivable has been employed to get the sharp points into the wire in a manner presenting the greatest obstacle to the trespasser, be it human or animal.

Some are designed just to scrape the hide off of you. Others to puncture you in as many places as possible if you touch it. Still another design is intended to grab and hold you (by your aching flesh) if you are so foolhardy as to try to climb over it. Anyway you look at it, barbed wire is antagonistic. Millions of miles of it have been used to contain herds of cattle and other animals, or to keep them out of certain areas. Other miles have been used on battlefields during the wars which constantly plague this planet, as a deterrent to attack from enemy soldiers.

Barbed Wire

One company in Colorado sells starter sets of lengths of ancient barbed wire, together with the patent dates and information. It is more interesting to look for your own. Anywhere in this entire country is a good place to find old and antique barbed wire. They have been strung, forgotten, and abandoned from one ocean to the other—in fields, in woods, on farms, and around town buildings. Sometimes you may only find a few inches still clinging to a rotting support or firmly nailed to the corner post of an old building, but a few inches are all that you need of species of wire to build your collection of relics of the varied attempts of men to guard their possessions from other men.

In fact, when we bought our property in the Catskill Mountain country many years ago, our deed was written with the various boundaries indicated. One boundary read, "— and thence West 105′–22″ for a distance of 745 feet to a *very old wire fence*." I recently took a leisurely walk through my "back forty" to try to find that marker, and sure enough— it was an old antique barbed wire strand. Only a few feet were visible, nailed to a couple of old trees, but it was there, together with new and obvious surveyor's stakes, quietly rusting itself back to the earth from whence the iron originally came.

Barbed Wire

Chapter sixteen

Stamps

★★★★★★★★★★★★★★★★★★★★★★★

Stamps

Postage stamp collecting is the largest and most popular of all hobbies. Many, many, millions of persons collect these attractive little bits of paper. Stamps can be purchased for from several for one cent, to over $250,000 for one stamp! More than any other item in our economy, stamps offer an education in the development of mankind.

One can learn from collecting postage stamps of the world, about the manufacture of paper, about colors and dyes, politics, government, currency, industry, sports, famous people, flags of the world's nations, countries long extinct and new countries just forming, animals and wild life of the entire world, flowers and fruits of the world, printing and engraving processes—there is literally no end to the things one can discover on the stamps of the different countries.

A great number of books have been written on collecting postage stamps. In fact, I have written one myself. Almost every hobby shop, department store, or stationery store sells stamps for collectors. Stamp dealers are in nearly every city and town in the country.

Besides buying stamps from dealers, you can find them on old letters and cards in attics and basements. Junk dealers are a good source of old papers having stamps affixed to them. You can write to pen pals in other countries and obtain stamps from foreign lands when they answer you.

Used stamps should be carefully soaked off the envelope or card—not torn off. Then they should be dried between clean white towels, or, better still, in a stamp drying book, which can be obtained at a very low cost from stamp dealers.

The large, cheap bags of stamps sold as mixtures for a dollar or less will yield sev-

Stamps

eral hundreds of different stamps to start a collection, and you can add to it by getting packets of stamps from countries you would like to fill in.

Keeping your stamps in protective albums will protect them from damage and soiling. You should never handle stamps without using stamp tongs. Fingers have an oil that could stain some stamps. Stock books having transparent pockets to hold the stamps is a better way than albums where the stamps must be held in with stamp hinges, especially for mint, or unused stamps. A stamp that has had a hinge attached is worth less than one which has never been hinged.

Many famous people in the world are stamp collectors. Our late President Franklin D. Roosevelt had one of the world's greatest collections. King George VI of England was an ardent stamp collector and his collection was worth an enormous amount.

Stamps

Chapter seventeen

Coins

★★★★★★★★★★★★★★★★★★★★★★★

Coins

While coins do not show the greatly varied scenes and pictures on their sides that stamps do, coin collecting is nearly as popular as stamp collecting. Coins are very much older than stamps. This is due to several reasons—

one being that paper was not invented until long after coins were minted. Another reason was that people did not send letters to one another in ancient times, but communicated by word of mouth.

Very early coins are crude affairs. They were made by taking a glob of metal, heated until it was soft, and hammering it flat between crude dies, each die having the head of a ruler or some symbolic design—an animal, or a bird, or some other symbol. Rarely were country names, dates, or values put on the coins. The dies from which early coins were made were usually as crude as the coin itself. The impression of the coin was practically never perfectly centered, and often part of the design on one side or the other was clear off the edge of the coin. Such coins are avidly sought after by numismatists the world over.

The early coins were made of iron, copper, bronze, silver, and gold. Large numbers of iron and copper kinds still exist, and bronze coins are plentiful. The silver and gold coins are more rare—probably because less of them were struck, and, because of their higher value, collectors are holding onto them.

Coins

Coins reflect the economic condition of their respective countries more than almost any other medium. The value of a country's currency is the mark of its economic stability. For many years the American dollar was the index of world value in currency. In recent times it has begun to decline in value, reflecting the instability of our internal economy. On the other hand, gold, which was established as a currency standard and for many, many, years, remained stable at about $35.00 per troy ounce, has begun to shoot up until at the time of this writing, gold is nearly $200.00 per ounce!

Naturally enough, this instability affects the value of the coins of a country, which in turn, affects their value as collector's items.

Our government manufactures coins in three major mints—Denver, Colorado; Philadelphia, Pennsylvania; and San Francisco, California. Coins minted in Denver and in San Francisco usually have what is called a mint mark on them. Somewhere on the coin is a tiny D for those minted in Denver, and a tiny S for coins from the San Francisco mint. Sometimes coins from the Philadelphia mint have a P on them, but not always, and usually, if a coin carries no mint mark, it was made in the Philadelphia mint.

There was, for a short time, a mint in Carson City, Nevada. This mint turned out silver dollars, but they were discontinued several years ago, and the stock remaining was supposed to have been melted down and reused. However, many thousands of the freshly made dollars were stored by the government

Coins

for some unknown reason, and for the last couple of years have been offered for sale to coin collectors at $35.00 each!

This is as deplorable an act as that of the government reprinting errors in postage stamps, since the Carson City silver dollars were a most desirable collector's item and worth a good deal of money. The act of selling off the hoarded dollars served to drop the value of *all* Carson City dollars in existence, and those hundreds or thousands of honest collectors who had paid a great amount for specimens for their collections now find the pieces have dropped to practically nothing compared with what they had to pay for them.

To keep your collection of coins, there are albums with holes or pockets to contain the pieces. Booklets for all kinds of United States coins are sold for a few cents each, and these will protect the coin from handling and surface scratches. Coins should not be handled with the bare fingers, especially valuable coins. The oil from the skin is liable to etch fingerprints into the surface of the coin which would be impossible to remove without damaging the coin itself.

Each year collectors can buy from the govenment a set of all the coins issued that year in uncirculated condition. These are put up in plastic cases, and sell for a little over face value. This way you can keep abreast of the current minting of coins, and obtain sets in perfect condition for a collection.

The condition of a coin is the index of its value, and every tiny scratch on the surface detracts from the value of the piece. Bright uncirculated or proof are the two most desirable conditions for coins. Bright uncirculated means a coin that has not been circulated to the public, and is bright, smooth, and shiny all over, with no marks or scratches. A proof coin is one that has been struck from a special polished die by the mint, and several of these are minted from each coin struck, as a general rule. They are initially available only from the mints, or from a government agency selling coins to collectors.

Coins

Chapter eighteen

Travel Decals
★★★★★★★★★★★★★★★★★★★★★★★★

*Travel
Decals*

Have you ever seen an automobile or a trailer with a large number of gaudy and colorful decals fastened to a window or door? These are the decals that every state in the country has, some states having many more than just one kind, and they are available at stops along the highways. Motels, restaurants, shops, stores, and novelty shops have racks of the decals from their locality. Decals are available from all the large cities within a state, offering a scene of local reknown or historical interest.

Actually, there are ordinances against fastening these decals on car windows, but practically no one pays any attention to the ordinance, and the law is not enforced, so one continues to see anywhere from one to fifty or more of the colorful posters plastering up a rear window.

A better way to keep the collection, since, when the car is finally sold or traded in, the decals cannot be removed, is to mount

Travel Decals

them in an album of some kind. A photograph album is ideal for the purpose.

Like other souvenirs, travel decals can provide a good way to remember a vacation trip, and they will recall those happy tours taken to the scenic spots of the country.

Besides advertising spots in the state and country, decals are made with so-called comic sayings, cartoon pictures, and other printing on them. These can be collected as a separate item, or as part of a decal collection.

An interesting wall plaque can be made by collecting a decal from every point you touch on a trip, then attaching these to a pane of glass in the order in which they were obtained. The glass then can be mounted in a frame to hang on the wall. The resulting conversation piece goes well with modern wall decor, and you can re-travel the trip because the decals are in chronological order on the frame. A different frame could be made for each trip you take, and the frames can be changed on the wall from time to time.

Travel Decals

Chapter nineteen

Buttonhooks

★★★★★★★★★★★★★★★★★★★★★★★

*Button-
hooks*

Today, a buttonhook is an extinct tool, but in the days when Great-grandmother was a girl, it was a very important article, and a necessity in every household. Shoes, blouses, gloves, all were buttoned up instead of laced or zippered, and, on a shoe, for instance, operating the buttons was a real struggle without the aid of the simple tool made for the purpose.

Some gloves, especially dress gloves, went up the entire forearm of the woman wearing them, and were closed with a long row of tiny buttons. It was almost an impossibility to button such a glove unless the wearer used a hook.

The collecting of these implements is a nostalgic thing, and to an older person, brings back memories of the hustle and bustle of getting ready to leave for the theater—"Where's the blasted buttonhook?" my father would shout, walking around with his shoes flapping open on his feet. Mother's wail of distress would be for her own glove hook, which she simply could not find—perhaps because I had filched it to hold my pigeon cage door shut until I made a new latch.

Buttonhooks were made of many different materials. The hook part was metal, of course, and the handles were everything from celluloid to gold and everything in between. I remember one on my mother's dresser with a handle of real tortoise shell, and one my sister's beau gave her with a handle of sterling silver. There was quite a family squabble when she got it. It was too personal a gift for a young girl to have accepted from a man.

An interesting incident concerning buttonhooks occurred when a friend once tore down an old building. Embedded in one wall he found about five hundred old rusty buttonhooks, thrown into the wall when it was being

Buttonhooks

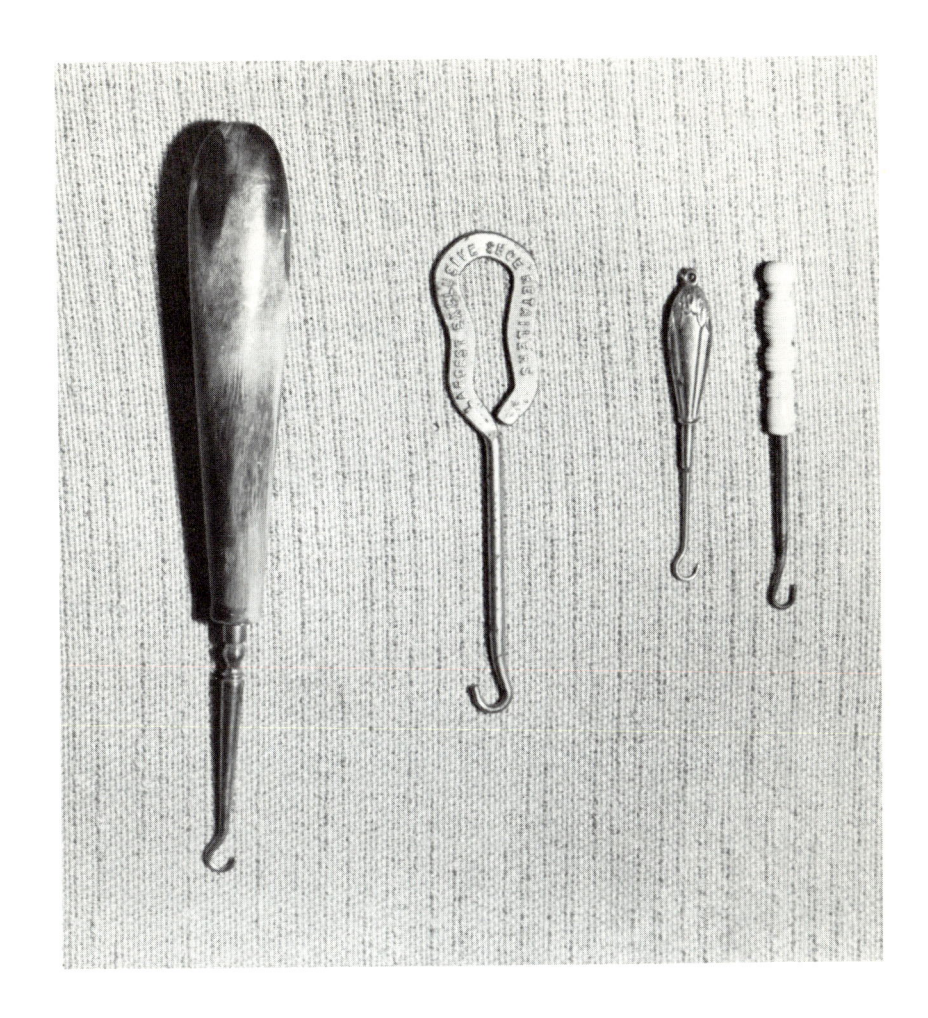

concreted up as a reinforcement. It developed, on inquiry, that the building next door had been a buttonhook manufacturing company when his place was going up. I suppose those used in the masonry were rejects for one reason or another.

Buttonhooks can be found hanging on nails in old barns, attics, anywhere at all. They were universally used for picking up things to pulling wire, besides the purpose for which they were invented.

Button-hooks

Chapter twenty

Shoulder Patches
★★★★★★★★★★★★★★★★★★★★★★

Shoulder Patches

Nearly every branch of civil service, military, police, and many civilian organizations, use colorful embroidered patches sewed to the shoulders of uniform shirts and jackets.

NEW YORK
EXCELSIOR
STATE POLICE
WOODSTOCK
NEW YORK
POLICE
MARYLAND GUARD · CSS VIRGINIA
41ST NATIONAL
20TH ANNIVERSARY
N-SSA
2ND MD. CAV. MAY 1970 2ND MD. ARTY.
MALLARD
SAUGERTIES, N.Y.
1970
JULY 18-19
120 TH N.Y.V.
NORTH-EAST REGIONAL SKIRMISH
KAYADEROSSERAS SKIRMISH
2ND
BALLSTON SPA, N.Y.
JUNE 8-9 1968
KAYADEROSSERAS SKIRMISH
BALLSTON SPA, N.Y.
JUNE 28-29 1969

The collecting of these patches is a popular hobby. Many of them are very complicated in design and embroidery, and a collection of patches of the state police departments of each state in the union would make an imposing display. They could also be obtained from city police departments, as well as sheriff's offices throughout the state counties.

Some departments do not like to let their patches be owned by an outsider, which merely makes it all the more exciting when you do get a patch from that department. Perhaps you can trade one of your locals for a different one, or someone you know is on the force which uses the patch you want. There are any number of ways to obtain them.

Shoulder patches are also used by organizations like the Boy Scouts and Girl Scouts; men's clubs like the Masons, Kiwanis, Rotary, and many others. Shoulder patches are even used by some companies such as delivery companies. Large private firms sometimes like their employees to wear uniforms and often supply shoulder patches, too.

Shoulder Patches

Chapter twenty-one

Bookmarks
★★★★★★★★★★★★★★★★★★★★★★

Bookmarks

Sometimes bookmarks are really works of art. I have seen them made out of satin, embroidered with a pattern that would do justice to fine table linen or a very special handkerchief.

Bookmarks

Bookmarks are designed to lie flat between the pages of a volume to keep the place of the reader without his turning down the corners of the pages. As a writer, such treatment of a book gives me a shudder of horror, but some people make a common practice of doing just that. Of course, "dog earing" book pages ruins the book's value, as well as causing actual physical damage to the work, and anguish to an author.

I suppose bookmarks have been in existence nearly as long as books, but nowhere have I been able to discover who was responsible for designing them at first. I have seen bookmarks in a museum made of thin sheets of gold, with the top end set with gemstones. Such a mark is a piece of jewelry, but it serves the purpose for which it was made, and it must be a source of pleasure to mark the page of a wonderful book with such a place marker. Silver has also been used for bookmarks, but the most commonly used material is thin fabric, thin leather, or heavy paper.

A few years ago I was given several bookmarks from Japan. They were made by laminating two thin sheets of plastic together, with butterflies in the middle. The wings of the butterflies were real, but the bodies had been removed and printed paper ones substituted because of the thickness of the insect's body.

The bookmarks were pretty enough to look at, but they were entirely impractical, because as soon as they had been in our climate for a few weeks they curled so badly that it was impossible to flatten them out enough to use them. A great many things made in foreign countries undergo this dimensional instability when brought to our country. The average climate sometimes differs so radically that changes in temperature and humidity make the item warp out of proportion. Sometimes the covers of books made in the Orient warp so badly that they have to be cut off and new covers made of material that is made for our own climate.

Many publishers of fine books build bookmarks right into the bindings. A length of narrow ribbon, usually of silk or satin, is sewed into the backbone or spine of the book in such a way that it may be placed between any of the pages as the book is read. Most Bible printers practice this method.

Bookmarks

Chapter twenty-two

Spoons

★★★★★★★★★★★★★★★★★★★★★★

Spoons

Nearly every exposition, big fair, and similar event has offered souvenir teaspoons as a memento of the occasion. The spoons, of course, were sold at the events, not given away free.

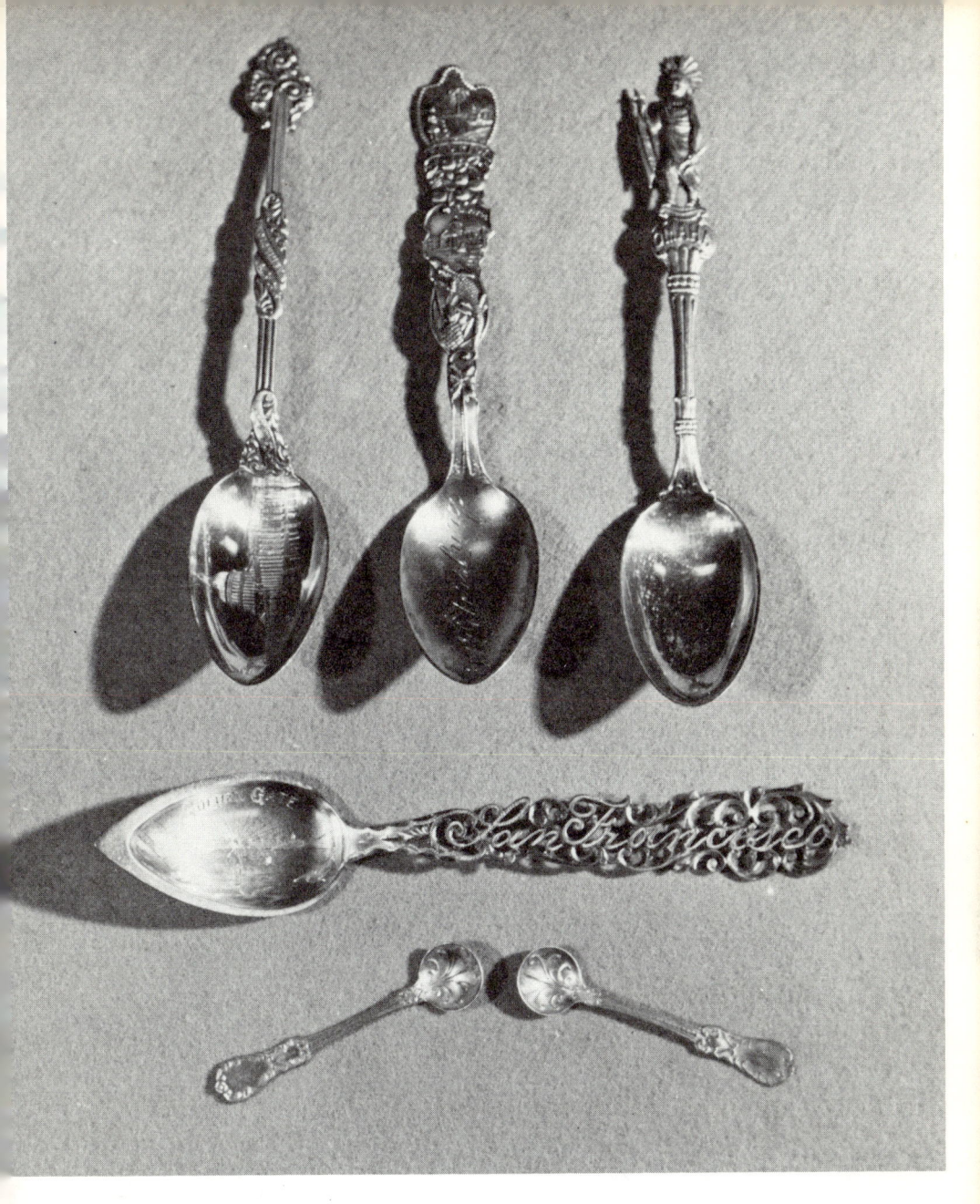

Some of them were made of sterling silver. The great majority of them were of silver plate, made the same way as the average table services were manufactured.

The handles bore a legend concerning the event, or perhaps a picture or one of the buildings at the fair. Some of them were pierced and quite ornamental.

The collecting of these souvenir spoons is widely practiced, and such items are eagerly looked for in old attics and cellars. Almost without doubt Great-grandma had a spoon or two among her treasures, which she kept in memory of her trip to one of the great fairs.

Usually these spoons were teaspoon size. Sometimes tablespoons were made, and also tiny salt spoons.

European fairs also had these kinds of souvenirs, and a wonderful collection could be made of world-wide events.

Spoons

Chapter twenty-three

Bubble Gum Items

★★★★★★★★★★★★★★★★★★★★★★

Not too many years ago someone who hated parents invented a messy, miserable concoction called bubble gum. Evidently he realized that no one would buy the stuff without some kind of inducement, so he enclosed with each gob of gook, a card, or a decal, or some other useless item. Free—when you paid for the gum.

Among the first of these items were cards upon which were printed the pictures of

Bubble Gum Items

popular baseball heroes, and, on the reverse, a little thumbnail biography of that person. Thus came into being a craze that swept the kids of the United States off their feet—baseball cards.

Since that time, a bevy of other kinds of things have been packaged with the ubiquitous bubble-gum chunk. The gum was even rolled out into flat slabs to accommodate the wrapper which could also enclose a card. Baseball heroes, hockey players—I have recently discovered a series devoted to different poses of David Carradine as Caine in "Kung Fu," the backs of which cards are parts of another picture designed to be assembled as a kind of jigsaw puzzle.

About the worst of these offerings are self-adhering pictures which the unsuspecting kids are roped into collecting in order to plaster their school notebook covers with them. These are, I guess, intended to be funny. Some of them are. Some of them are sick. Almost all are named after a famous and well-known product, but with the name caricatured. Ghoulish Mummy Tee Shirts made by Fruit of the Tomb; Spills Brothers Coffee; Footsie Rolls; the number of these stickers seems countless, but the kids go for them like a horse goes for oats.

As a matter of fact, in one of the major hobby magazines, each issue carries ads asking for these bubble-gum cards—offers to buy, sell, and trade, so the fad is nationwide. Also, considering the cost of the ads, the collectors of these items are not even kids any more, but their fathers (and/or mothers)!

Bubble Gum Items

106

Chapter twenty-four

Toy Soldiers

★★★★★★★★★★★★★★★★★★★★★★

Toy Soldiers

Here is an item that has had a long history. Toy soldiers have been the delight of small boys for many, many decades. They were first made in Europe, and the very finest ones are still made in England.

The cannons were wonderful. All of them were replicas of actual cannon used by the armies of the different countries, and they really worked, shooting BBs by releasing a spring-loaded plunger in the barrels. The cannon balls had just enough power to knock a soldier or two off his feet.

The soldiers themselves were works of art. Beautifully cast of lead, they were carefully painted in the exact colors of real uniforms, and, on most of them, something moved. The arms or legs were movable, and some of the heads turned. Some were mounted on prancing horses, others were made in kneeling or bent over positions, to place at the breeches of the artillery in a lifelike pose.

Toy soldiers were made in the United States, too, but they were much cruder in execution, the uniforms were not nearly so exact, and the whole toy was of inferior workmanship. The tiny details that made the individual pieces so much more exciting were not included in the American soldiers as they were in those made in Europe.

Every army of the world was available, African native troops, Indians, ancient Persians, and Egyptians—all were represented in the parade of the nations on my bedroom floor.

I remember well when I was in my pre-teens spending long and fascinating hours sprawled out on the floor of my room, my battalions of toy soldiers lined up ready to do battle against one another. My father used to bring new regiments home to me every time he went on a business trip to France, England, or Germany.

Chapter twenty-five

Autographs

★★★★★★★★★★★★★★★★★★★★★★

Autographs

  Of course, everyone knows about autographs. Collecting them begins almost as soon as a boy or girl is big enough to hold up a notebook and pen to every famous person coming to town. Movie stars, political personages, foreign visitors are all deluged with requests for their autograph.

Historical autographs are also much in demand. Most popular are autographs of Lincoln, Washington, Jefferson, and all people connected with the development of our vast country, its government, its politics, and its civil and foreign relations.

Autographs can be collected in small notebooks made for the purpose. They are called autograph books, and the idea is that each autograph obtained occupies one entire page. These are the little books which autograph collectors hold out to celebrities for their signatures.

Another way to collect the desired names is on letters and documents signed by the important persons. In the autograph book the celebrity can, and usually does, write some remark, witty saying, or personal comment as well as sign his name. Most collectors like this method best. However, the autograph book limits the collector to those persons who are living and who he is able to meet face to face. Collecting autographs on letters, cards and documents widens the field considerably, and permits the acquisition of a far greater number of more famous people.

Autographs

Chapter twenty-six

Thimbles
★★★★★★★★★★★★★★★★★★★★★★★

Thimbles

In this modern day and age far fewer people do their own sewing than in the old days. However, sewing is still quite popular and hand sewing still a good part of making one's own clothing. When a person hand sews, a thimble is often used.

The purpose of thimbles is two-fold. The first, and major function is to provide a rigid and slip-proof surface with which a needle can be pushed through heavy or resistant fabric. The second function is to keep the eye of the needle from puncturing the tip of the sewer's finger.

A utility thimble is merely a small cup of metal designed to slip over the end of the finger, with a band and top end covered with tiny indentations. The end of the needle slips into one of these indentations and is pushed through the fabric without slipping off.

Thimbles

According to the way the person sews, either the end of the thimble or the side can be used. Usually the end is brought up against the needle, since this method gives the longest stroke of the finger. However, in quilting, the stitching is a curious sideways kind of thing, and quilters most generally use the side of the thimble. For that reason, you will often find thimbles without any ends in them. These are quilting thimbles, and it takes good craftsmen to use them without driving the needle clear into their fingers.

Thimbles are made as souvenir items, for sale at fairs, expositions, and other large events. Sterling, gold, aluminum, just plain steel, even ivory and bone have been used to make thimbles. Some of them are works of art, hand painted around the borders, built up by hand of precious metals, with complicated designs worked into them, or with a legend inscribed around their borders. However they are made, and whatever they are made out of, every thimble serves the same functions, and every thimble must have a series of indentations somewhere on its surface in order to be of service.

Thimbles

Chapter twenty-seven

A List of Things People Collect

★★★★★★★★★★★★★★★★★★★★★★★

*A List of
Things People
Collect*

One volume could not begin to list all the things collected and cherished by the human race. It would, indeed, be a check list of every artifact known from antiquity to the present time. In this chapter a list has been compiled of collectibles. They have been taken from hobby magazines, collector's catalogues, auction lists, and similar sources, and, as nutty as they may sound, someone is collecting each of the items listed herein. The list is by no means complete. One could fill an entire book with lists of things collected. Some of these items cost many dollars each—some hundreds of dollars, and some, thousands of dollars. Almost no matter what amount is asked for the item, if a person collects them, someone is willing to pay the price.

Acetylene Lamps
Advertising Pencils
Andirons
Antique Furniture
Arrowheads
Automobiles
Automobile Coins

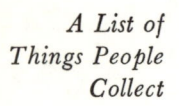

A List of Things People Collect

Automobile Horns
Automobile Hub Caps

Balls
Barber Bottles
Beads and Beadwork
Beer Cans
Beer Steins
Bells
Bicycles
Birds' Eggs
Birds' Nests
Books
Book Ends
Bottle Caps

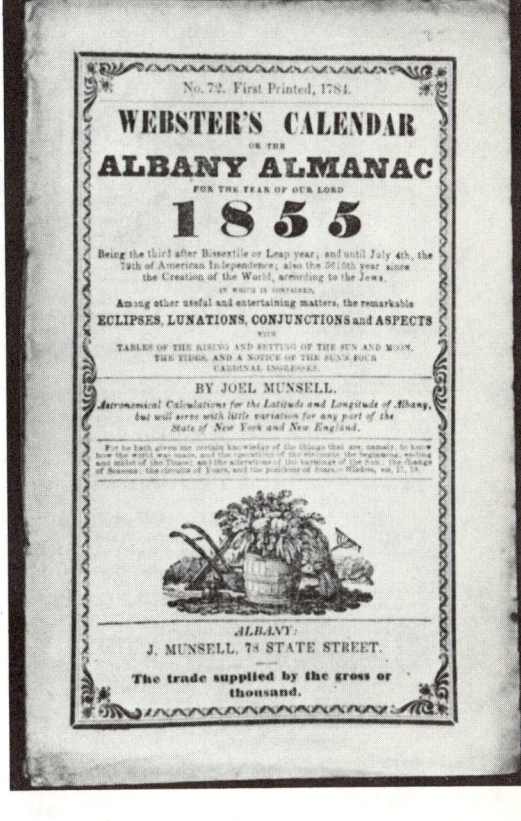

Bottle Labels
Bric-a-Brac

Cabinet Hardware
Cameras
Camera Lenses
Candle Holders
Candle Molds
Candle Sconces
Canes and Walking Sticks
Cannons
Casting Molds
Catalogues
Centennial Coins

A List of Things People Collect

Chess Sets
Cigar Cutters
Clocks
Clothing
Chamber Pots
Coats of Arms
Coca-Cola and Root Beer Trays
Cocktail Stirrers

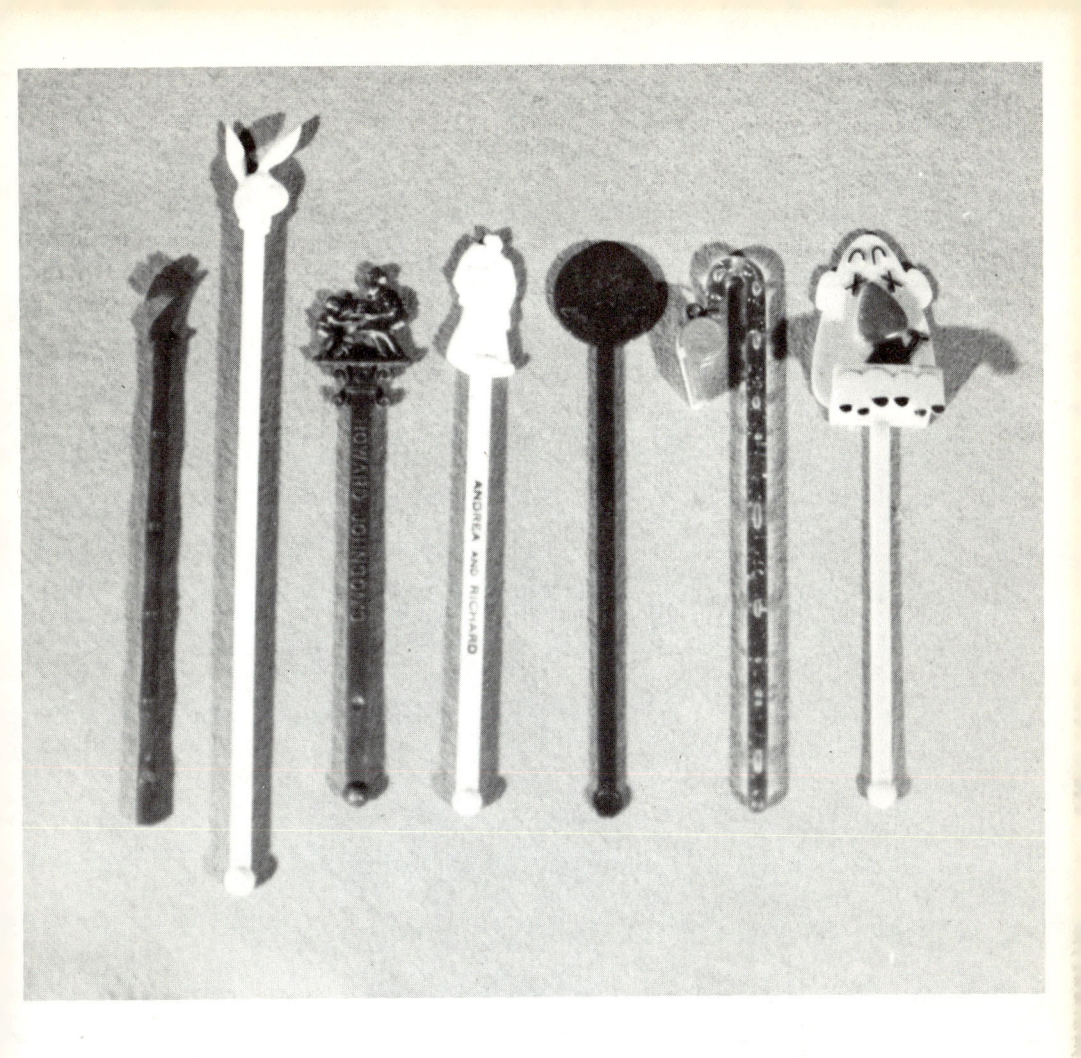

Combs
Convention Items
Coverlets
Cruets
Crystal Radio Sets
Cuff Links
Cups
Cut Glass

Dental Equipment
Dolls

*A List of
Things People
Collect*

Dollhouses
Door Knobs
Door Knockers
Drafting Instruments

Early American Silverplate
Egg Cups
Electric Light Bulbs
Electric Trains
Empty Cartridge Cases
Erector Sets

Fabric Samples
Fish Flies
Flags
Fountain Pens
Furniture Casters

Game Tokens
Glass
Glass Lantern Slides
Gloves
Guns

A List of Things People Collect

Hair Brushes
Halloween Masks

Hand Mirrors
Horseshoes

Indian Relics
Inkwells

Knives

121

Lanterns
Lantern Slide Projectors
Letter Openers
Lockets
Lodge Items

Magazines
Magnifying Glasses
Maps
"Match Box" Toys

Marbles
Measuring Spoons
Mechanical Banks
Merchandise Tokens

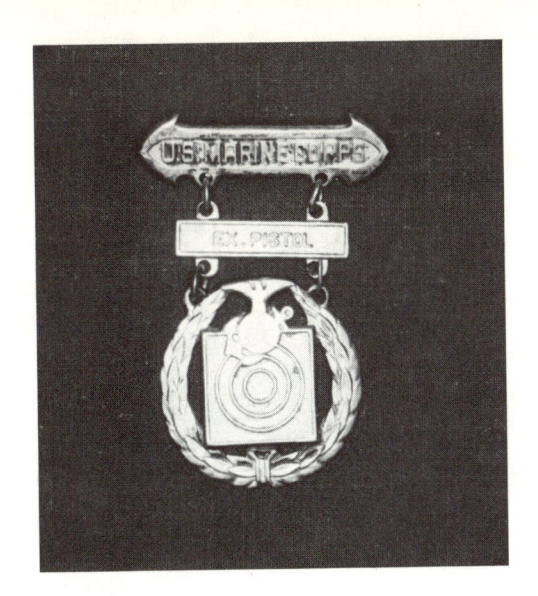

Military Objects
Milk Bottles
Miniatures
Model Airplanes
Movie Films
Music Boxes
Music Rolls

Nails
Napkin Rings
Neckties
Needlepoint
Netsukes
Nutcrackers

Oriental Rugs
Ornamental Ticket Punches

Padlocks
Paperweights
Perfume Bottles
Pewter
Phonograph Records
Pins

Pipes
Place Mats
Plates
Playing Cards
Police Items

*A List of
Things People
Collect*

Political Items
Porringers
Presidential Coins

Radio Tubes
Railroad Spikes

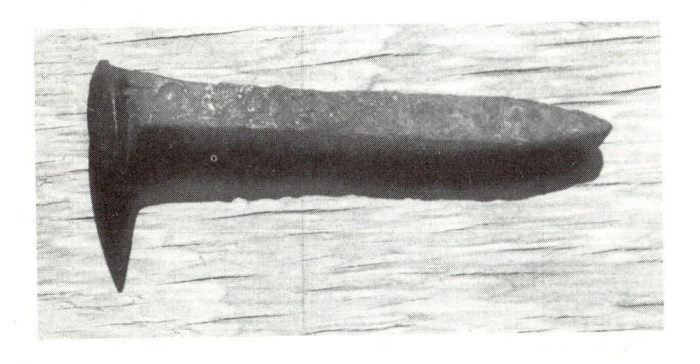

Salt Shakers
Saucers
Scales and Balances
Scissors
Scrimshaw
Sealing Wax
Seals
Sewing Machines
Sewing Machine Bobbins
Sewing Thread Spools
Shaving Mugs
Sheet Music

*A List of
Things People
Collect*

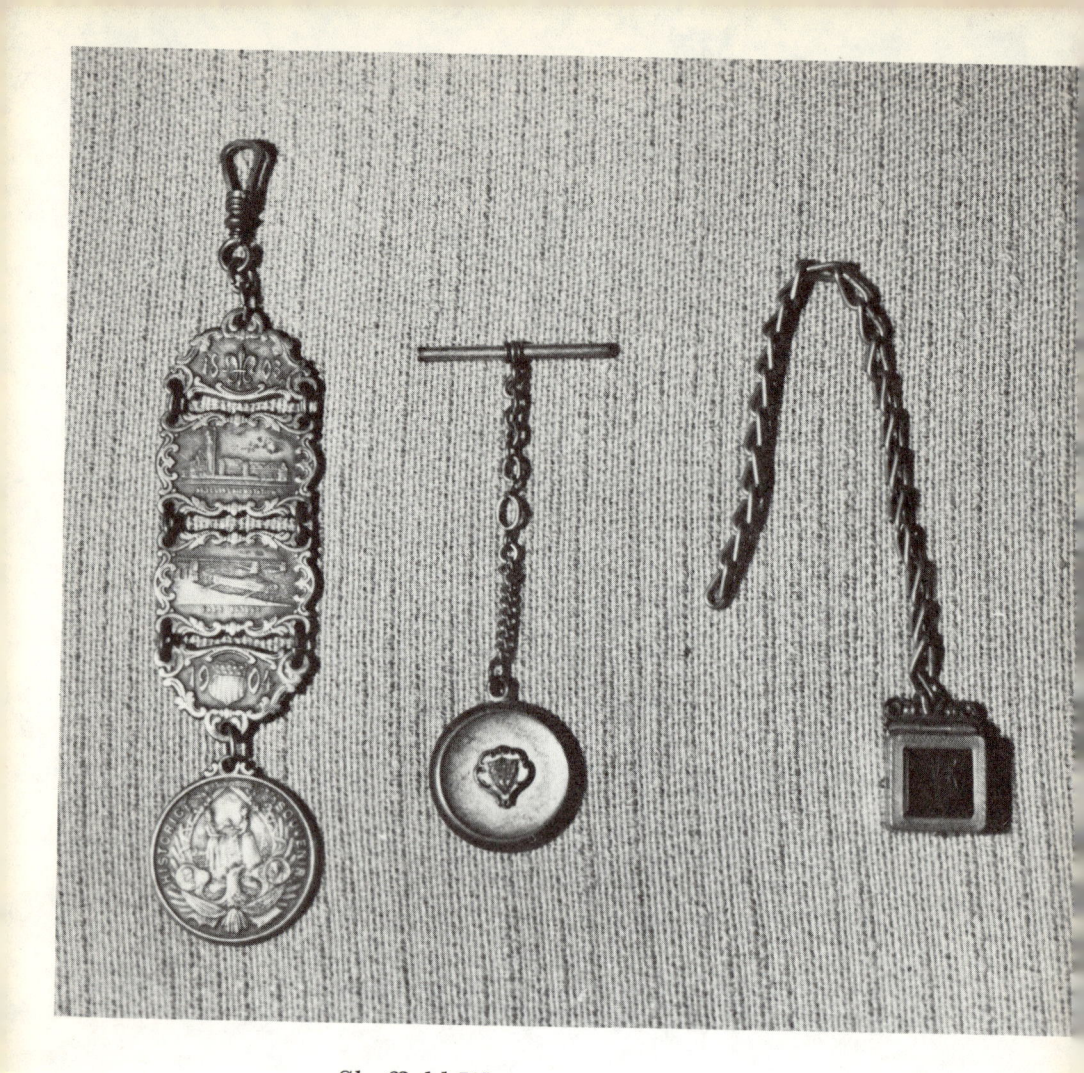

A List of Things People Collect

Sheffield Ware
Soup Tureens
Spectacles
Sugar Picture Eggs
Surgical Instruments

Tea Caddies
Telephone Directories
Thermometers
Tie Pins
Toothpick Holders
Toy Stoves

Transportation Tokens
Type Founts

Umbrellas
Umbrella Stands
Upholstery Nails

Valentines
Veterans Organization Items

War Relics
Watches

*A List of
Things People
Collect*

127

Watch Fobs
Water Pitcher and Bowl Sets
Windup Trains
Wood Blocks
Wooden Nickels
Woodworking Tools
World's Fair Souvenirs

*A List of
Things People
Collect*

PAUL VILLIARD, author of COLLECTING THINGS, was born in Spokane, Washington, and, before his death in 1974, lived in Saugerties, New York. Although he started out as a mechanical engineer, he soon found that his real talent lay in writing and photography.

He traveled for many years in the Pacific Islands, South America, and throughout the United States. From these years of traveling, observing, and photographing, came much of the material for many of his books.

An avid collector himself, Mr. Villiard's other books include COLLECTING STAMPS, WILD MAMMALS AS PETS, REPTILES AS PETS, INSECTS AS PETS, BIRDS AS PETS, and EXOTIC FISH AS PETS. His beautiful photography and fine writing have appeared in *Natural History, Audubon Magazine, Popular Home Craft, Home Crafts and Hobbies, Reader's Digest,* and *Nature and Science* magazine, among others.